A DIVERSITY OF
verse

Ron Steele

A DIVERSITY OF verse

Ron Steele

MEREO
Cirencester

Mereo Books

1A The Wool Market Dyer Street Cirencester Gloucestershire GL7 2PR
An imprint of Memoirs Publishing www.mereobooks.com

A diversity of verse : 978-1-86151-632-9

First published in Great Britain in 2016
by Mereo Books, an imprint of Memoirs Publishing

Copyright ©2016

Ron Steele has asserted his Right under the Copyright Designs and Patents
Act 1988 to be identified as the author of this work.

This book is a work of fiction and except in the case of historical fact any resemblance to
actual persons living or dead is purely coincidental.

A CIP catalogue record for this book is available from the British Library.

This book is sold subject to the condition that it shall not by way of trade or otherwise be lent,
resold, hired out or otherwise circulated without the publisher's prior consent in any form of
binding or cover, other than that in which it is published and without a similar condition,
including this condition being imposed on the subsequent purchaser.

The address for Memoirs Publishing Group Limited can be found at
www.memoirspublishing.com

The Memoirs Publishing Group Ltd Reg. No. 7834348

The Memoirs Publishing Group supports both The Forest Stewardship Council® (FSC®) and the
PEFC® leading international forest-certification organisations. Our books carrying both the FSC
label and the PEFC® and are printed on FSC®-certified paper. FSC® is the only
forest-certification scheme supported by the leading environmental organisations including
Greenpeace. Our paper procurement policy can be found at
www.memoirspublishing.com/environment

Typeset in 9/15pt Bembo
by Wiltshire Associates Publisher Services Ltd. Printed and bound in Great Britain by
Printondemand-Worldwide, Peterborough PE2 6XD

Contents

The Traveller I
An Autumn Day
Caitlin, the courage of a child
Dreams
For me: a eulogy for Ronnie
God Bless You Mam
To Margaret with love
Olive #1
Respectful Thoughts
Seaside & Grandkids
Season (winter)
Season's thoughts
Sleep, perchance to dream
Spring
Stress
The Ghost Train
The lady with the auburn hair
The old house
Thoughts
When I was a kid
Wind chimes
Number Five May Avenue
A declaration of love
A Frostways bus ride
A seasonal tale
A winter's tale
Always believe in angels
Anniversary
Bygones
Children
Dreamy
Friends
God, a perception of
Kids
Leslie
Lonesome
Love
Love's Dedication, to Margaret with love
My reason to be
My Mum, Olive
My Wife
NZ
Olive #2
That night
The mirror
The Toad
The Traveller II
Thinking time
Weep not for me
Who cares?
Winter bygone
A summer's daydream
Anguish of a dream
Conflicts
Parkinson's (the curse)
Remembrance
The last poppy petal
When you dream

The Traveller I

The breeze gently stirred the autumn leaves
on the branches of a lonely moorland tree.
An afternoon sun with a pale saffron glow
would give way to night in an hour or so.

But. while it shone, stark beauty around,
as a lone weary traveller tramped over the ground.
He had little time to admire the scene
of a majestic landscape, gold and green.

As slowly he wended his weary way,
dark clouds were gathering at the end of the day.
At the pale light's fading the air grew chill,
he caught his breath atop a windswept hill.

No longer majestic this moorland scene,
black and grey replaced gold and green.
As the rain started to fall from an angry sky,
he hoped the storm would pass him by.

But the rain drove down in stair-rod form,
and he was many miles from the safety of home.
Brigands and thieves would perhaps gain from his plight,
But would they be out on such a foul night?

With the light now gone and his way unclear,
he wished he were anywhere but right here.
Shrugging his shoulders, he even managed a grin,
perhaps he would find a wayside inn.

On he stumbled over gorse and stone,
a rain-swept figure on the moor alone
caring little that he was an awful sight,
bedraggled and wet on this stormy night.

The time dragged by in hours it seemed,
to keep the cold out he began to dream.
He dreamed of summer and bright blue skies,
same shade of blue as his beloved's eyes.

Long sunlit walks through flowery fields,
the warmth of the sun on their faces they'd feel.
He and his love would often dream,
whilst dangling their feet in a cool meadow stream,

Suddenly back to reality he came
when his footing he lost in the pouring rain.
Tumbling down in the heather and gorse,
a little bruised but none the worse.

On against a howling wind and driving rain,
he searched for the path, but 'twas in vain.
He'd made this journey several times before,
but which direction was home he was not sure.

He battled through the ceaseless storm,
exhausted, wet, and chilled to the bone.
Weary with the effort of each foot put down,
then suddenly, his feet were on level ground.

Was this the path, the one he'd sought?
but his mind was clouded with uncertain thoughts,
At least his step was a little easier now,
but he must find shelter, somewhere, somehow.

Without a warning a dark shape loomed tall,
he found himself standing beside a stone wall.
High, grey, foreboding and grim,
no way of knowing what lay within.

Shuddering, he gathered the last of his strength,
and followed the wall along its great length.
Finally reaching an open gate
but a gut feeling inside made him stop and wait.

Through the gate he could see a form,
somewhere to shelter, but was it safe, dry and warm?
Was it a ruin, or the devil's lair?
his mind was racing while standing there.

As he pushed the gate wider, it screeched sharp and loud,
as the moon came out from behind a dark cloud.
The rain had ceased and the stars shone bright,
the building stood stark in the pale moonlight.

With ramparts and windows like castles of old,
and roughly-carved gargoyles, silent and cold
A long flight of stairs led to the front door,
on which was a knocker that he'd seen before.

His footfalls were loud as across the courtyard he stepped,
the sound echoed around, but his nerve he kept
But on reaching the door he started to shake,
should he knock, or perhaps just an entrance make?

If this was a ruin there'd be no one home,
but standing there he did not feel alone.
He reached for a knocker that was monstrous in size,
but before he could touch it the door opened wide.

A loud creak echoed as the door swung back,
he stepped through the portal, though real courage he lacked.
He'd never thought himself brave before,
as he stood in a hall on a cold stone floor.

This didn't seem like a ruin, the house appeared to be sound,
there were paintings and tapestries all around.
It was cold and damp as if unaired,
and yet there were candles lighting the stair.

A great long staircase curving around,
high stone walls from the roof to the ground.
Apart from the trappings it was furnished stark,
as the end of the staircase disappeared in the dark.

"Hello", he called, "Is anyone there?"
his voice echoed back from the top of the stair.
He stood very still and strained an ear,
he held his breath to control his fear.

The sound of the wind as if down a chimney stack came,
whistling and howling, it brought back the rain.
The rain he could hear back through the great door,
splashing the threshold in a consistent downpour.

At least it was dry and out of that downfall,
standing alone in this great lofted hall.
But was he alone? Unlikely, thought he,
if this house was lived in, where could everyone be?

Off to his right was another great door,
and off to the left were several more
Each one enormous and sturdily made,
like sentinels silently guarding a tomb or grave.

He could not decide which door he should try,
or wait for an answer to his echoing cry.
"Hello", he called again, "Is anyone there?"
At last came a sound from the top of the stair.

He was not sure who or what had made that sound,
but it seemed to reverberate all around.
A cold draught of air moved across his face,
as his whole body shook, he felt his pulse race.

The sound came again, this time clearer it seemed,
it was now that he prayed he would wake from a dream.
This sound from the top of the shadowy stair,
made his flesh creep and bristled his hair.

The great hall fell silent as his brain whirled around,
trying to recognise that familiar sound.
In the stillness he waited holding his breath,
not knowing for certain how much life he had left.

Then in an instant, from he knew not where,
the smell of wet dog filled the air
Scratching and scraping of canine claws
came swiftly towards him without a pause.

With all the speed of a lightning flash,
from out of the shadows it made a dash.
Pouncing upon him before he could move,
wild blazing eyes, and fangs dripping with drool.

Whilst holding the beast back by its collared throat,
the smell of its breath almost made him choke.
As he stared into the fire in its bloodshot eyes,
he felt himself weakening against its tremendous size.

The strength he had mustered was almost spent,
oh how he wished he'd had time to repent!
Then, just as he was about to let the beast have its meal,
from somewhere in the darkness a voice shouted, HEEL!

In an instant he felt the danger had passed,
too weak to move, he just gave out a gasp.
Trying to come to his senses, it seemed,
had that voice had saved his life, or was it a dream?

Then in the half light as he turned his head,
he came face to face with his recent dread.
Sitting at his side drooling, and almost unreal,
was the hairy beast that had nearly had him for its meal.

Seeing this beast now an obedient hound,
made him relax as he lay there on the ground.
Regaining his composure, he became aware
of a tall dark figure at the top of the stair.

Slowly and carefully to avoid aggravating the beast,
in total silence he got to his feet.
Gingerly he took a step back away from the hound,
snarling still as its head swivelled round

ITS HEAD SWIVELLED ROUND!
the head had the movement of a tawny owl.
Somewhat unnerving, this curious sight,
one more thing on this frightful night.

Whilst his head was trying to make sense of it all,
there came a sound from down the dark hall.
A sound he had heard a half minute before,
this time it was louder and many times more.

He could neither run in fear for his life,
nor stay in fear for that very same life.
Feeling that his end was surely now nigh,
he clenched his fists and prepared to die.

Fearing the worst, he held his breath,
wondering with a pounding heart what would happen next.
He could tell from the sound of the snarling and scratching,
there was more than one of the hounds sat guarding.

After what seemed an age, though probably not so,
the beast at his side rose, and moved slowly across the floor.
It moved a few feet forward in a silent flow,
as though to face an oncoming foe.

With his attention drawn once more to this oncoming rush,
he felt his body would be completely crushed.
These hounds from hell were almost upon him,
a way out of this he could not imagine.

Maybe help from the figure at the top of the stair?
but a quick glance told him he was no longer there.
Then out from the bowels of hell, or so it seemed.
came all the furies that had ever haunted his dreams.

Three, four, or, possibly more,
just like the one he had faced before.
Now it seemed, this one was standing its ground,
with backs to the wall they faced these fiendish hounds.

He felt the stone wall behind him with a clammy hand,
the other hand fell upon an old candle stand
Gripping the metal firmly, he swung it around,
and started a sweeping motion just above the ground.

Swoosh, went the great metal stand as it cut through the air,
like the sound of the scythe from the grim reaper.
As the beasts attacked the metal struck home,
sending one flying in a mass of bloody hair and broken bones.

Squealing and whimpering it writhed on the floor,
and gone was the sound of its blood-chilling roar.
As he turned he could see his partner was fighting the other three,
this could be his chance to flee.

The thought had barely crossed his mind,
when he dismissed it as being so unkind.
He could not abandon this beast so brave,
for now, this new friend he had to save.

With no other thought than to save his friend,
he brought down the stand on the back of another fiend.
He heard a sickening crunch as the metal bore down,
squealing like a stuck pig was this disabled hound.

Of the two that were left, one broke free,
he could tell by its wounds that it could barely see.
But it came slowly towards him snarling and dripping blood,
in the background he could see his friend's position was not good.

But before he could help, he had a fight of his own,
it was now or never, if he was ever again to see his home.
With bristles erect on its hairy back,
the snarling beast crouched ready to attack.

Bracing himself for what could be the last fight of his life,
he began to think of his love, his late wife.
Would she be proud to know he had stayed?
would she think that he had been brave?

In an instant his thoughts were snapped back into place,
as the beast made a leap, aimed at his face.
with all the speed he could muster he blocked this vicious hound,
as he trapped its bite with the iron bar, he was forced flat to the ground.

With blood and drool dripping down on his face,
he hoped he could die with all good grace.
Then, just as he felt he was about to breathe his last,
a sudden flash across his eyes past.

In a frantic howling and snarling, the beast was thrown from him,
off to his right there was a whirling mass of blood, hair and din.
Struggling to his feet he tried to help but couldn't get in a telling blow,
how to end it he did not know.

Then, just as if he was given a sign,
his friend rolled over as if resigned.
This was when he took his chance,
he struck the beast's head without a second glance.

With a long drawn out moan it slid to the floor,
the last fiend was dead; it was quiet once more.
His relief turned to sadness at the bloodstained form,
that of his friend lying still, crumpled, tattered and torn.

He knelt quietly down beside this former foe
lifting gently its head from off the cold stone floor.
Its eyes with a look no longer a bloodshot red,
but a pale blue of spring flowers shone out instead.

Its eyes rolled back to its skull within,
and its lip seemed to curl in a sort of half grin.
With a heavy sigh it passed away,
this noble beast had had its day.

He did not know why it had stood by his side,
and chosen to fight instead of run and hide.
But he was grateful on this fateful night,
that it made the choice to stay and fight.

Laying his friend's head gently down,
he stood up slowly and looked around.
Then dragging a tapestry from off the wall,
he carried his friend's wrapped body down the great hall.

To his surprise it was almost dawn,
the sky was clearing to a beautiful morn.
Walking round to the courtyard's rear,
he found a small garden, where a patch he cleared.

He placed his friend in a crudely-dug grave,
it was best he could do with a rusty old spade.
Saying a prayer, he shed a tear,
on the grave of a friend, a friend so dear.

Sighing, he thought it was time to go
as the sun came up with a soft warm glow.
Back through those gates now, not so foreboding and grim,
out on the road, hoping to find a wayside inn.

Walking along with a now weary tread,
how he wished he had somewhere to lay his tired old head.
But just as the thought had come to mind,
he heard a sound in the distance far behind.

High on a hill, against the sun's bright glow,
he thought he saw two shapes, he'd seen before.
Then, on the morning breeze, there came a howl,
not frightening at all, more like that of a lost soul.

A tired smile broke his dirty face,
as a hand he rose to shield his gaze.
In the distance there, upon a rise,
he thought the light was playing tricks with his eyes.

After a while he recognised the forms,
it made him smile as he headed for home.
He knew now his journey would have a safe end,
as he waved goodbye to the ghosts of his wife and friend.

An Autumn Day

Gone is the summer's warmth of bright colours' glare
heralds now the coming of winter's chilling air.
The trees cast down their golden carpet upon the ground,
and rooks above their nests in heady flights around

Misty pale sunlight shines through shady groves,
it glistens now on wet muddy roads.
The cool winds rise, dry the flower's dewy kiss,
and blow away the curtain of silky mist.

Clouds from the west in angry billows grow,
and shroud the sun's pale saffron glow.
Darkening skies then falling rain,
bring longings for summer to mind again.

Holidays have all gone, the sea's cold spray's upon one's face,
castles of sand trodden down, with a thousand footprints in their place.
Above the hollow sound of seagull's caw,
foretelling the approach of winter's roar.

The sea's hue, once green, has taken on a brackish grey,
as it now blends with the horizons far away.
As the clouds race headlong, running before windy gusts,
broad shafts of light through a grey ceiling rush.

Billowing swirls like rampant steeds on sunbeam legs
over hedgerows vault and wide streams leap.
The noonday sun with a warming hand
caresses all things as it sweeps o'er the land.

A welcome warmth to plants, trees and all things green,
and the hurrying and scurrying of every creature seen.
They cannot gather food for a winter store too much,
to guard against Jack Frost's icy touch.

The sun arcs swiftly across the sky,
it's orange glow less harsh to the eye.
The air is cooler now as the sun goes down,
on hilltops pausing, like a golden crown.

No twilight chorus from summer birds,
above the trees and chimneys heard.
Footsteps echoing in silent streets,
on shiny wet pavements are the hurrying feet.

This autumn day that is now almost past
will become a memory, and only memories last.
Reflecting as the years go by in season form,
our summers had known a greater warmth.

As the winter's edge draws ever nigh,
another season has all but slipped by.
Sitting beside the embers bright,
untouched by the coolness of the night.

Staring through the flickering flames,
remembering people, faces and names.
Have the fates been kind to those you knew,
do they have visions of your face too?

With hopes that the dawning of tomorrow's day,
will bring golden beams, sparkling and gay
To stave off for a while the seasons change,
making time for us all to rearrange.

Sitting by the fire to keep out the cold,
one gets a chill to the bones as one gets old.
So at the drawing of Jack's icy veil,
we will begin a winter's tale.

Caitlin
The courage of a child

When we speak of courage we always think of soldiers brave and bold,
but there is in life a greater strength, if only truth be told.
Angelic face and smiling eyes, a laugh that melts your heart,
will always bring you comfort, now your world is torn apart.

The courage of a little girl not knowing much of life,
puts to shame those of us who think that we have strife.
It's often said a leap of faith is for the old and wise,
but truly, faith's within the blue of those two smiling eyes.

One so young has not the concept of there being a heaven above,
only a belief in fairyland, which was the thing she loved.
For one so young to have such faith is indeed a gift so rare,
it can only come from one who was raised with tender loving care.

Even though the thought of Caitlin's smile will often bring a tear,
let her courage give you strength as you journey through the years.
No one can hope to understand the pain that you must feel,
but we know that through experience, the heart will slowly heal.

So when that emptiness inside feels like a heavy stone,
always remember that her love made a house a home.
It can never be the same it's true, as each memory away is filed,
as parents you can take great pride in the courage of your child.

All our love to you all and our thoughts are with you
Margaret, Ron, and Craig
In memory of a beautiful and brave little girl - Caitlin.

Dreams

In the slice of death that I call sleep,
where my mind departs to a world of dreams
It's hard to grasp reality's tail,
when my soul is in limbo, or so it seems.

Visions of the past so crystal clear,
surreal formations in my mind's eye.
Is there another world to which we're bound?
or just a nothingness when we die.

I am not fearful of death itself,
it will hold no dread when my time is nigh.
But I fear that my mind one day I'll lose,
one thing in life I hold so high.

The very essence of who I am
is held within my mind
My fear is that I'll lose control,
and leave myself behind.

The memory of each dream fades fast
when I awake upon the day.
But in moments when I'm feeling tired,
back into my thoughts they oft times stray.

I recall small parts of what I've dreamt,
with feelings most insecure.
I always question if they are for real,
and somehow I'm never sure.

Mixing reality with what one dreams
for some means little at all,
But for me it's a torment within my mind,
and my mind's my very soul,

I could not exist without free thought,
or the means to question why
One's mind is all that there is left,
as the years go quickly by.

The end to my life matters just as much
as all the years before.
Because what is the point if I do not know,
the ones that I love and adore?

If I become a mindless shell,
I hope that God is kind.
Shining his light on those I love,
and the ones I leave behind.

All the love that I have had
has made me what I am.
Through all the years, and all life's trials,
I have been a lucky man.

I could not have come thus far I feel,
without a true and caring wife.
She has always been my one true friend,
throughout our married life.

I hope that I'll lose not my will,
when it's time to say good bye.
I also pray I'll be aware,
when the end is drawing nigh.

If at that time, I'm of sound mind,
do not for me a teardrop cry
For I'll thank God for the life I've lived,
and fear not to say goodbye.

For me: a eulogy for Ronnie

I have left this earthly body,
this worn and shrivelled frame
I have left this terrestrial home,
where once I had a name.

My life was nothing special,
no heroic deeds did I
Perhaps I may be called to mind,
in the future, by and by.

Within the space of my allotted time,
many things I sought to do.
Mistakes I made as did everyone,
like most, there were quite a few.

I never felt at any time,
that I'd been cheated out of life.
My world was always full of luck,
with Margaret as my wife.

She shared my hopes and all my dreams,
in my life she shared the strain
A wife and mother so steadfastly
she bore our children's pain.

For me this life has flown so fast,
so much unsaid and done.
My hope is that in the future years,
this world will be a better one.

So as I depart this world,
laid to rest at last.
There is a hope that I will not be
a forgotten memory of the past.

2nd. February 1944 - ?

God Bless You Mam

Though your body's now an empty shell,
your spirit is flying free
No longer racked with earthly pain,
or with eyes too tired to see.

So many years without Dad's guiding hand,
so many years alone.
But now together at last again,
where heaven will be your home.

You leave behind an empty space,
and a pain that will be slow to ease
But for you it's been a long hard road,
now at last you can rest in peace.

For you our love was left unsaid,
until you were near the end
But I knew you were trying to say goodbye,
when with love you squeezed my hand.

That brief moment I will never forget
until the day I die.
It will comfort me all my life,
when each time a tear I cry.

You'll stay forever within our hearts,
the memories will never pass.
But we know your now in a happier place,
you've found your peace at last.

Good night God bless Mam.

NZ

Beyond the hills of green there lies
a sea that's blue to match their skies
With air that's clean and fresh to breathe,
and trees that never brown their leaves.

This land where the sun is strong and bright,
a land of a billion stars at night
Where seldom is seen a fall of snow,
and winter's face barely makes a show.

Nature here moves gently along,
in rhythm the tui's song.
There are no creatures savage or wild,
the creatures there are gentle and mild.

Golden sands, or sands of black,
sights of beauty there is no lack.
Mountains, hills and silver ferns,
Breath-taking views at every turn.

This land is far better than one could dream,
for where but a dream, could there be such scenes?
Primaeval beauty beneath one's feet,
so close to nature one feels complete.

Beauty it's said is in the beholder's eye,
the beauty here is land, sea, and sky.
Created with love by a powerful hand,
God bless and defend New Zealand.
until the end of time.

Respectful Thoughts

Amid these rolling hills of green
larks on high o'er this peaceful scene.
Silent white sentinels row on row,
in fields where bright red poppies grow.

All is quiet where once was war,
this peace we have the cost they bore.
No one can say what would have been,
if we had lost these fields of green.

Gravestones silently standing tall,
each one marking where the brave did fall.
someone's son, or someone's père,
though years ago their grief we shared.

We shed a tear in true respect,
the only payment brave men expect.
They cared not for medals and bands,
just a whispered prayer as we clasped our hands.

And with each prayer there'll always be,
a soul that's loved and now set free.
Away on high where larks do soar,
above fields where bright red poppies grow.

Seaside & Grandkids

The waves curl over and come crashing down
the seagulls cry and hover above.
This east coast sea is a murky brown,
And the wind brings a tear to the eyes of my love.

Holding hands, and with collars turned high,
strolling the empty promenade
Whilst clouds race across an angry sky,
the November rain starts falling hard.

We hurry to the car as the weather we curse,
but I really don't mind the rain
We've had better, and I suppose we've had a lot worse,
after all, it's autumn that's here again.

Through steamy glass we survey the scene,
and remember those past summer days
When the sun was warm and the trees were green,
and the grandkids not so far away.

When I was young I never dreamt,
I'd travel very far from home.
To the coast was as far as I ever went
no thoughts that in distant lands I'd roam.

I'd rarely dream of things I'd do,
or wonder what life I could create
But life sped past, and the things I knew.
have now come and gone, all but too late.

We marvelled at seeing our child's first steps,
all too soon she has children of her own.
The passing of time we'll not regret,
for we know we made a house a home.

Now she lives on the world's far side,
far away from the place we call home.
New Zealand is where she now resides,
it's good to hear her voice on the phone.

But it's no substitute for holding her near,
or holding the grandkids in your embrace.
Even though older now they are so very dear,
no longer children, but young adults now with their own space.

In the past we've never realised or even thought,
that we'd have a broken heart to mend
But with memories that can't be bought,
we have a love that will never end.

Season (winter)

Trees stand stark at break of day,
from a night that's long to end
They groan to greet the morning sun,
when icy winds their branches bend.

By day the sun's an eerie light
as if from a candle glow
But soon those winds like wolves will howl,
and turn the winter rain to snow.

Silent falls the pure white shroud,
all over hill and dale
A time when life's exceeding slow,
and winter's sun shine's pale.

Sharp winds that give a watery eye,
loud footfalls on the frozen snow,
shadowy forms with collars raised,
wearily trudging, homeward go.

A welcome lantern from a window beams,
as moonlight glistens upon the snow.
There's heard the singing of seasonal rhymes,
of remembered yuletides long ago.

Beside the fire burning bright,
warming the chill from one's old bones
With the door firmly closed against the cold,
one's safe and sound within one's home.

Stars like diamonds on black velvet shine,
against the cold night sky
across a silvery moon,
silently clouds float on by.

But soon the long winter's night is o'er,
and the wind does stills its moan
A pale morning sun above the church roof rises,
with a sleepy eye we wearily greet the dawn.

As sure as night follows day the summer will return,
but first spring will once again burst forth all around.
The melting of snow and ice slowly brings
a new life's abundance that shoots up from the ground.

Warmer and longer the days grow now,
as the sun climbs higher in the sky.
Joy and love for everyone,
With no longer a winter's teary eye.

Season's thoughts

White cotton buds on azure blue
golden brown against a carpet green.
Cold fresh breeze o'er the morning dew,
nature's recipe for an autumn scene.

The wind moves the creaking boughs,
the blue skies are turning dark.
A rook's caw is heard above the windy roar,
long gone summer's sweet song of the lark.

Grey skies of flurrying snow
swirling in biting icy winds
Tears down cheeks about to flow,
as winter's grip begins.

Silent falls the pure white shroud
that covers hill and dale.
it falls from dark grey clouds,
and makes children's faces pale.

The sun is always slow to rise,
upon a winter's morn.
Little warmth comes from its glow,
it makes the old folks groan.

To thaw the frozen ground,
takes time, that, in itself stands still.
The old folks sigh with eyes that roll around,
as they feel the winter's chill.

There is always a quick end to the day,
it's dark before you know.
The winter nights will slowly pass away,
but not before the fall of more snow.

Not as bad as the winter of forty-three,
the old folks oft times say.
We can only say what will be will be,
for we do not have the longevity for that sort of card to play.

To take each day as it comes around,
is all we can hope to do
To make the best of what's laid down,
and pray that we will always come through.

The seasons come and the seasons go,
warm days in summer and cold in winter.
We cannot alter what the weather will show,
it is not natural that we interfere.

So long as the spring will follow on,
we need not fret about the cold.
Because we know that before too long,
we will not care, for we'll be old.

Sleep, perchance to dream

When you dream, do you dream of fresh green fields,
of cows and sheep, and all things real?
A clear blue sky, a babbling brook,
a warm summers day, or a classical book?

Do you dream of the sun upon your face
or of a sweet white wine you long to taste?
Waving corn and cotton-bud clouds,
a song in your head you want to sing out loud?

In a dream you can be whoever you choose,
no luck required, you cannot lose.
Rich man, poor man, beggarman, thief,
create a world that's beyond belief.

In your dreams you can with eagles soar,
or with lions hunt and hear their roar
With creatures great, and creatures small,
your place can be beside them all.

The shrill note of a lark high above a green meadow,
or a golden sunset that makes one mellow.
On a mountain high, or vast open plain,
on the stormy seas of the Spanish main.

Hearts and minds that are truly free
can be wherever they want to be
With heart and mind, you can free your soul,
from a body upon which life has taken its toll.

The beauties of life can be in your head,
even though your body is tied to a bed.
A dream must be shared with someone who'll care,
who'll beside you stand and always be there.

You don't have to be there to see a sunrise,
the glow can be felt if you just close your eyes.
Experiences are gained from the day you are born,
and with love in your heart you're never alone.

But when morning comes and dream's laid aside,
and you feel all that you have is only your pride.
All the riches of the world are not enough,
to ever replace the one that you love.

That one you feel is the whole of your life,
whether that one be a husband or wife.
No matter whatever your fate will be,
your love can bridge eternity.

Spring

When winter's grip is lessened
and the March roar is but a purr
You can hear if you stand and listen,
spring's songbirds as they take to the air.

Fading now is the rook's rasping caw,
as buds appear on the leafless trees
Now's the time to see other birds soar,
above the grassy leas.

Spring's sunshine brings forth the flowers gay,
of daffodils, crocus, snowdrops and the like
They erase from our memory a harsh winter's day,
with their varied colours bright.

Each creature seeks warmth from springtime's sun,
each plant its flowers to bear
New life everywhere has just begun,
the glow of springtime's everywhere.

We look forward to summer that's not so far away,
the memory of winter will not last.
The weather's warmer by the day,
as the time flies by so fast.

Babbling brooks and meadows green,
waving reeds against skies of blue
Create a bright and welcome scene,
with colours of a vivid hue.
The warmth of the sun's glow,
will warm the cockles of your heart.
Soon we'll see the wheat fields grow,
with stacks upon the haywain's cart.

As we meander through the fields of green,
my love and I embrace.
Those pale blue eyes are the prettiest ever seen,
as the sun's reflection in her angelic face.

Stress

Stress is relative to each, to everyone a different pain
In this busy world, the day's, end will soon be reached.
But surely with the passing of time, the stress will come again.
If only we could slow time's dash and savour life's pleasures full
if we could go at a regular pace, and not disaster make.
Then mayhap we would avoid the crash that besets the troubled fool.

There are few who find a perfect peace, rarer still the time to contemplate,
So in this world of life's treadmill, stop, and take just one small breath.
This stress for many will never cease, but for a few the hope will reincarnate.
If you don't you never will experience all of life's wonders before one's end,
you will make enemies and friends in this world as you in life progress,
but that is the way of life it seems, and heartaches we have to mend.

So don't take heed of those cynical types who say that we are doomed,
just live your life as best you can with your loved ones true.
Then you can say with hand on heart that you did the best you could,
and take strength from the fact that you and yours owe naught to anyone,
having done no man injury or wrong, we can walk proudly through life,
be good to each man you meet, then you'll have the respect of everyone.

The Ghost Train

Tom stepped from the cab in the old station yard,
it was cold and damp with not a soul about.
The ground still wet, it had been raining hard,
the night felt strange, there was no doubt.

He turned to the cabbie to pay his fare,
but was startled to find that he stood alone.
The horse and carriage were not there,
just the wind he heard through the trees made moan.

Tom could not explain what had occurred
as he shook with the cold, or was it fear?
He stood still and listened, but nothing stirred,
not a sound save the wind came to his ear.

No sound of hooves galloping away,
no rattle of wheels on cobblestones.
No crack of a whip or horse's neigh,
just the feel of a chill right through to the bone.

Tightening a muffler around his throat,
he approached the station's booking hall.
Lifting the collar of his long black coat,
he bought a ticket at a hole in the wall.

There was something strange as he paid his dues,
all he could see were the clerk's two hands.
Barely a glimmer from inside shone through,
for the window was barred with rough steel bands.

The clerk didn't speak as the ticket he gave,
the hands took the money with no sound at all.
No pleasant remark or gesture made,
as the ticket was passed through the hole in the wall.

Placing the ticket inside his coat,
Tom picked up his case and stepped through a door.
Tightening a muffler around his throat,
he was out on the platform into the night once more.

Along the platform was a waiting room,
poorly lit, but with a fire in the grate,
In the corner, a man sat alone in the gloom,
and a clock on the wall said the hour was late.

Saying 'Good evening' and raising his hat
Tom placed his case upon the floor,
But the man, who was well dressed, round and fat,
Tom's cheery good evening seemed to ignore.

Tom pulled up a chair close to the hearth,
and began rubbing his hands before the flame.
The man in the corner was of considerable girth,
it was hard not to notice as Tom proffered his name.

There was no real answer, except for a grunt
from beneath a black broad-brimmed hat
with hands clasped across his waistcoat front,
he reminded Tom of a fireside cat.

As the clock on the wall ticked noisily on,
the fire in the grate crackled and hissed.
At the clock's chime Tom knew something was wrong,
it appeared by the time several hours he'd missed.

Excuse me sir, is that clock correct?
he asked of the man in a puzzled tone
but the hairs on Tom's neck fairly stood erect,
when with a shock he realised he was all alone.

As with the cab outside, there was not a sound,
nothing to betray the man had moved at all
But as the thoughts in Tom's head whirled around,
a voice from outside began to call.

'Eleven forty-five to Chester-Le-Street'
said a voice in eerie tones
Tom moved to the door, but with two lead feet,
as the voice continued its drone.

Opening the door, Tom heard a rush of steam,
as on to the platform he gingerly stepped.
Was this real, or was it a dream?
looking into the haze what should he expect?

As the steam in the air slowly drifted away,
there before him was a terrible sight
Only a few feet distant, and as clear as day,
a vision that made his face turn white.

The ghostly outline of a battered old train,
stood at the platform hissing steam.
The doors then opened, and from the carriages came,
spectral shapes in a continual stream.

Dozens of spirits in a silent throng
walked around or through him, as if he weren't there.
In a time and a place, he felt he didn't belong,
afraid and trembling, transfixed he stared.

Down from the train in a skeletal form,
stepped the driver, waving a bony hand.
Motioning, it seemed, to him alone,
to climb upon his footplate stand.

This death's head vision had red glowing eyes,
and about its frame a ragged uniform
Gleaming white teeth that seemed to smile,
and draw him closer into the unknown.

Slowly forward he was compellingly drawn,
toward the spectre standing there.
He could not speak, not even a moan,
as the foulest stench then filled the air.

This ghoul before him then made a bow,
and with fearful dread Tom climbed aboard the train.
Beads of sweat formed upon his brow,
as the wind rose high and it started to rain.

Without a word the ghoul nodded its head,
whilst a bony hand opened the firebox door
Then. with gleaming white teeth and eyes glowing red,
motioned for Tom to cross the floor.

Struggling hard to resist a hypnotic stare,
that came from those two red glowing eyes,
Tom felt his very flesh being stripped bare,
as in his brain poor souls in torment cried.

He felt he was facing the fires of hell,
and his skin began to blister and burn
When would this end? How could he tell?
and of his fate, from whom could he learn?

Closing his eyes, he tried to offer a silent prayer,
though in truth he didn't know what to say
He pleaded to someone, something, somewhere,
to forgive him and grant him another day.

Dragged toward to the fire inch by inch,
Tom began to smell his own singeing hair.
He tried not to scream, or even flinch,
as in to the face of death he stared.

At the moment he felt he could endure no more
and this was all that his body could take.
He sank to his knees upon the floor,
as his shoulders began to tremble and shake.

This shaking grew stronger, and stronger still,
then a voice called his name, whispering in his ear.
To react to this call took the whole of his will,
for Tom's very soul was still racked with fear.

The voice became louder within Tom's brain,
as with an effort he raised a weary head
Then he realised he was not on the train,
but sat by the waiting room's fire instead.

The gentleman in the broad-brimmed hat
was firmly shaking Tom's limp pale frame.
On waking with a start from where he sat,
he saw that the hem of his coat was in flames.

Removing the coat quickly he stamped out the blaze,
with relief he sighed, then wiped his brow.
Not thinking clearly, as though in a haze,
His mind began to question the where and the how.

Looking at the clock, he asked is that right?
turning to the man in the broad-brimmed hat.
But once again he got a fright,
for there by the hearth was a large black and white cat.

Confused and troubled he tried in vain,
but in his mind was unable to get things straight.
So on with his coat and out into the rain,
his decision was not to travel that night.

In the station yard he caught a cab,
on getting home he went to bed.
During the first real night's sleep he'd ever had,
his terrible ordeal never entered his head.

The morning sun streamed onto his bed,
as he awoke refreshed to meet the day.
He drove last night's happenings out of his head,
but was it a dream? So who could say?

After breakfast Tom walked to the end of the street,
not a soul about on this beautiful day.
No friends to hail, no one to greet,
all was quiet in such a strange way.

Turning the corner, he heard a cry
from a paper boy across the way.
He crossed the road and passed close by,
to read on his placard the news of the day.

The news on the board made him turn quite pale,
the words, large, bold and in plain sight:
'RAIL DISASTER AT THORNTON-LE-DALE',
but the date was only last night.

RON STEELE

Buying the paper Tom quickly read,
a report of the crash from a man on the scene.
The date and the time were going round in his head,
was last night real or was it a dream?

Reading on, the news became grave,
it appeared on that night no one had survived
Only one creature last night had been saved,
a black and white cat pulled from the wreckage still alive.

The owner it seemed of this black and white cat
had perished with all who had been on the train.
He was described as a man in a broad-brimmed hat,
who sheltered by the fire from the pouring rain.

The report told how the train had left the track,
on a night when storm clouds hid the moon
When in driving rain and at the thunder crack,
the engine crashed through the wall of the waiting room.

At the stroke of twelve when the disaster occurred,
Tom was leaving the old station yard
But the sound of the wind was all he had he heard,
so making sense of this had his brain working hard.

Deep in thought Tom wandered home,
his mind in turmoil about the man in the hat.
Had he been by the fire alone,
or in the company of a large black and white cat?

What would have happened if he'd not left that room?
or had he ever been there at all?
On a night when the storm clouds hid the moon,
it seems that he and fate had a very close call.

On reaching home he heaved a sigh,
it was just a dream and leave it at that.
When something at his window caught his eye,
sitting there was a very large black and white cat.

The lady with the auburn hair

She glided silent through the morning mist,
with a flowing white veil and skin so fair
Across lawns that held a dewy kiss,
she was tall and slender with auburn hair.

Through trees and shrubs of leafless form,
her spirit was seen both night and day
She wandered the grounds with an air all forlorn,
along leaf-strewn paths she wended her way.

This spectre held no fear when seen,
her soul it seemed was earthly bound.
A vision angelic, as if from a dream,
it wandered the paths all through the grounds.

In her youth she did give her heart
to a soldier who was both brave and bold
With a vow to her love that they'd never part,
for theirs was a love to have and to hold.

She shed a tear as he went off to war,
and each day to him a letter she'd write.
His portrait she kept hanging by the door,
with a hope he'd always be safe from the fight.

From battlefields in a land far away,
whilst holding a picture of his lady fair
He wrote with love, a letter each day,
keeping safe a lock of her auburn hair.

Three long years she did wait alone,
the time she'd pass walking through the grounds.
Hoping each day was the day he'd march home,
she tended the flowers as each season came round.

Then it came one bright spring morn,
with trembling fingers, and a beating heart
a letter she held, by a courier borne,
this small sealed note she then tore apart.

With trembling hands the note she read,
in action lost as the armies engaged.
Was that all there was of her love to be said?
through tear-filled eyes she stared at the page.

In grief on her knees she sank to the floor,
a million tears she cried that day,
Something inside her had died in that war,
in a foreign field so far away.

As the weeks went by she grew pale and drawn,
though some did try, she was not consoled.
In her silent room she wept all alone,
for her love who was both brave and bold.

One warm summer's evening as the moon rose high,
a young woman in white, slender and tall,
As a million stars lit up the sky,
was seen on a rooftop before her fall.

No one knew if she'd jumped to her death,
as her spectral form's seen both night and day,
But it's clear there was little in life for her left
though eerie, her form's still beautiful, they say.

Then late one summer as the shadows grew long,
A figure appeared near the garden wall.
As the blackbird began its evening song,
there stood a soldier straight and tall.

It was good, he thought, to be home again,
but the joy in his heart soon turned to grief
As he slowly walked with the aid of a cane,
the tears in his eyes were of disbelief.

When told that his love had passed away,
he took on the look of a man frail and small
His face became drawn, and his hair turned grey.
and he no longer stood so straight and tall.

All he'd endured had taken its toll,
his spirit though brave was torn apart.
With no fight left he became weary and old,
living the rest of his life with a broken heart.

And now sometimes at night when the moon is high,
he sees his love walk through the garden alone
While a million stars light up the sky,
through flowers and trees, of a place they called home.

One day their spirits will be entwined and they'll never again part,
for on that day their souls will be forever free
Joined by love, and with one true heart,
they'll be together again for all eternity.

The Old House

The old house creaks and sometimes moans,
it seems to have a soul of its own.
As I stood and stared at the empty street,
the rain against my window beat.

In that street on the cobbles cold and damp,
eerie pools of light from old gas lamps.
The house has stood for many a year,
and once was filled with joyous cheer.

But now it's a dark foreboding place,
so many harsh winters it's had to face.
The paint has peeled and the timber's bare,
I wonder why I'm still living here.

In the distance a clock struck the hour,
I remember wishing this night was o'er.
But as I stared down through a watery pane,
I saw a figure alone in the pouring rain.

It stood beneath an old gas lamp,
on glistening cobbles cold and damp.
As I fixed my gaze upon the figure below,
with its form ensnared in the lamp light's glow.

Tall and broad this figure did stand,
purely by stature it must have been a man
Dripping wet, and in a dark hooded cloak,
strangely this sight brought a lump to my throat.

Silent and still the figure stood,
of him I saw little, just the top of his hood.
Perhaps he waited for a friend to meet,
cold and damp down there on the street.

Then suddenly the scene was as bright as day,
from a lightning flash not far away.
Then the familiar rumbling sound,
as suddenly the storm seemed all around.

Another bright flash across the sky,
for a moment there distracted my eye.
I returned my gaze to the street below,
but no figure stood in the lamp light's glow.

No sight or sound of his hasty retreat,
no sound in the night of hurrying feet
Only the sound of the pouring rain,
alone once more with my thoughts again.

Sitting in the shadows of my dingy room,
the glow from the gas fire barely lifting the gloom,
Then from the hall, the front door creaked,
I called, who's there? But no one did speak.

I held my breath and strained an ear,
I called again - Is someone there?
Cold beads of sweat on my brow now formed,
on this stormy night in the house alone.

I called once more, Is someone there?
to my horror a creak upon the stair.
My heart began to pound in my chest,
the room grew cold; I could see my breath.

RON STEELE

Another creak, I locked my jaw,
I stared transfixed at the bedroom door.
The old brass handle began to turn,
as I felt my dry throat begin to burn.

Slowly the door creaked open wide,
and something in the shadows stepped inside.
Across the room I saw only a shape,
tall and broad in a long dark cape.

With no word uttered it closed the door,
turned, and moved slowly across the floor.
The hooded figure which bore no face,
made no sound as it crossed the empty space.

I could not move from my window seat,
like pieces of lead now were my feet
This thing drew close and I closed my eyes,
hoping this nightmare would pass me by.

Though I did not look, its presence I felt,
then slumping down, at its feet I knelt.
Gritting my teeth, I lifted my gaze,
and stared into the void where there should be a face.

He raised a hand without a sound,
as a mist began swirling all around.
This gesture made, I was compelled to stand,
he bore no flesh upon his hand.

I closed my eyes as I rose to my feet,
a second later, I looked, we were down in the street.
I stood in the rain and I felt the cold,
was there more of this nightmare yet to unfold?

Once more I gazed into that empty space,
where beneath that hood there should be a face.
His bony hand he raised yet again,
dripping wet in the pouring rain

A skeletal finger, he pointed across the street,
about I turned, shuffling my two sodden feet.
How strange, he pointed to the window of my room,
which I could just make out through the dismal gloom.

Suddenly there came a lightning flash,
the window pane burst with a tremendous crash
Shards of glass came tumbling down,
hitting the cobbles with a tinkling sound.

Then with a roar my room was ablaze,
whilst I in the street in a total daze.
In only a minute the whole house was a light,
in tall orange flames that were licking the night.

Then people came running to where I lay,
as the flames made the night as clear as day.
I stood and watched as folks gathered round,
a body – that was me! – laid there on the ground.

How could this be so? How could it be?
if I am here, how can that be me?
maybe things are not what they seem,
it could be me, but in a dream.

But if it's a dream, then why do I feel,
the rain and the cold, they are so real?
Once again I viewed the space,
beneath the hood where there should be a face.

How could I know what this creature felt?
as soaking wet at his feet I knelt.
Shaking, shivering and all alone,
what would I do now without a home?

With a rain-soaked face I stared at the flames,
and wondered if my life would ever be the same.
It was then I realised my life wasn't anything at all,
in fact, that's probably why I was all alone.

What cheer did I bring to my fellow man?
did I really do the best that I can?
So many things I could have done,
so many things I should have done.

I should have made my neighbours feel glad,
and not been content with what I had.
Not knowing what brings the joy of life,
being self-centered after the loss of my wife.

She was my world, she was my life,
more precious than gold was my wonderful wife.
She would not have wanted this shameful scene,
she never liked anyone nasty and mean.

But how can I change what has been done,
how can I go back to being a different someone?
Another flash of lightning over my head,
the reflection of flames in the pools so vivid red.

The rain continued in a torrential flow,
but what could I do? Where could I go?
I seemed to be nailed fast to the ground,
whilst a hive of activity went on all around.

People scurrying to and fro, shouting and calling my name,
can't they see me lying dead in the light of the flames?
What is the point of all this haste
when all of my life has been a waste?

The figure in the cloak again raised his bony hand,
and pointed to where I lay on the ground.
Only I was not there upon that rain-soaked street,
no body lay prone at a crowd's feet.

My brain whirled trying to make sense of this scene,
when from my house there came a scream
Not one of terror, but one of gladness,
as the figure stepped aside I viewed the madness.

my neighbours carried a body from this hellish inferno,
from my house to the street below.
With tender care they laid the body down,
cries of 'he's alive!' rang out all around.

As I watched in complete and utter disbelief,
this body that was me began to stir in the rain-soaked street.
Then another flash of lightning and the scene disappeared,
I was back in my room shaking with fear.

Rushing to the window, I held my breath,
looking down at what I might see, life or death?
But, as I gazed out of my window pane,
the night was clear, and gone was the rain.

Turning wearily, I sat by my window,
I could not believe the scene below.
with the setting sun glinting through the pane,
it was a warm dry evening with no sign of rain.

I could have passed it all off as a bad dream,
but I felt different, or so it seemed.
after a night I will never forget,
I was left with feelings of deep regret

Regretting the utter waste of my life,
my thoughts turned to my beloved wife.
What would she have said was wrong,
if she were not so many years long gone?

It's quite a few years since that fateful night,
when after a scare I saw the light.
The house though old is bright and gay,
there is no hint that it's seen better days.

The house is now warm and filled with love,
I know it's blessed from heaven above.
When the time comes to join my wife,
I will never forget the night that changed my life.

Thoughts

I stood atop a windswept hill,
watching the clouds race angrily across the sky
Then sat upon a grassy knoll,
whilst my life flew past, in my mind's eye.

I did not feel the wind's cold bite,
or notice the watering of my eye
As I sat there on that grassy knoll,
whilst I watched my life pass swiftly by.

Remembering sights and faces plain,
but their names so hard for my recall
Where and when, I know time and place,
in my mind's eye I see it all.

The sky grows dark as it's done before,
a gathering wind makes stout boughs creak
At a distance far, a rumble heard,
and from sky to earth a lightning streak.

The swirling wind brings forth the rain,
a rhythm strong and beating fast.
A freshness to the air it brings,
as I remembered in times past.

The thunder crashes all around,
like Chinese gongs it fills the air
Then lightning with thunder coincides,
as all the heavens it seems to tear.

The angry noises soon subside,
and a brightening of the sky at last,
Sunlight dapples yonder fields,
and the storm is almost past.

The highs and lows within one's life,
are often by some seen as a score
But win or lose, take what life gives,
for life's too short, and will soon be o'er.

When life's gone shed not a tear,
for you have had your time.
That piece of living that you call life,
has been a gift sublime.

A gift from who, or what, of your beliefs,
for everyone has their own God
A deity of whom they serve,
and a back to bare one's rod.

If we controlled our own destiny,
we could not live our life.
There could be no real order in this world,
only a chaotic one, that would be full of strife.

So if we take each day as it comes round,
there will be a reward somewhere
Even if it's only just,
in the way somebody cares.

Having someone care for you,
is a boon without compare
For someone's love is a precious gift,
even greater when it's shared.

The only thing that I can say,
that has ever been more profound
Is the love that you can give
to a child with your arms wrapped around.

So if you can leave this legacy,
your memory will never die
You will live forever,
in some loved one's mind's eye.

When it's time to cast off this mortal coil,
and take your place with loved ones past
You will have somewhere else your love can be,
where it will forever last.

When I was a kid

When I was a kid I and my friends,
played football in the street
with not many cars and bikes back then,
it really was a treat.

Every evening in the summer time
when the day was nice and cool,
and even after ★dinner too,
before we went back to school.

Sometimes we'd play upon waste ground,
where houses once had been
but they were bombed back in the war,
just as I came on the scene.

I couldn't wait for Saturday
when I'd play football for my school,
our team would beat most everyone,
not just cos I played in goal.

Through cold winds raw and pouring rain,
we'd kick that ball around,
we didn't mind the slimy mud
when we fell to the ground.

I still have a picture of that football team
back then in fifty-three,
the bestest team to ever come,
from good old Chapman Street.

As we moved on through other years
and played for other teams
we never had the same success
the way it once had been.

When we were twelve, our school came down,
and we were moved away
to Charterhouse, went most of our team,
to run out our last schooldays.

It never was the same again,
when we played rugby league
there never was the same team spirit,
the way it once had been.

Sometimes wishes come true, most times they don't,
but life goes on regardless no matter what
you do the best you can, whether it is right or wrong,
and you have to carry on with the little that you've got.

Looking back, I oftimes wish that I could be transported,
back to the time when life was slow,
and I was very young and innocent of life,
and as kids we knew very little of the road we had to go.

If I knew then what I know now, I've heard the old folks say,
would I have done things differently? I guess we'll never know.
I have only one wish, now that I am old,
that is to live just long enough, to see great grandkids grow.

*dinner: Yorkshire for lunch, 12 noon

Wind chimes

I stand atop a windswept hill
and stare across a valley green
Whilst clouds race by the sky above,
and shroud this winter's scene.

Cold air that bites like savage beasts
upon pale cheeks of wan
A numbness deep within my bones,
as I stand here all forlorn.

The sky grows darker as I watch
the twinkling lights below.
Lights in houses unaware,
soon comes the fall of snow.

A soft sprinkling of the purest flake,
a white carpet on the ground.
Nothing is heard except the wind
when the silent snow floats down.

Then soon the wind has lost its rage
and its teeth have lost their bite.
Clouds glide across a starry sky,
and unveil a moon so bright.

My breath I see in crisp clean air,
plain in the moon's bright gleam
As I gaze down, from atop a chilly hill,
upon this winter's scene.

My mind goes back to yesteryear,
to a time so long ago
When as a child I'd often play,
in fields of purest snow.

A time when time itself stood still,
no past nor future yet
A world within a child's mind's eye,
that with age we soon forget.

No thoughts but those upon that day,
no dread of years to come
Only the joy of living then,
until that day was done.

Each season brought a different joy,
in weather warm or cold
As a child it made no difference then,
unlike now that I'm old.

My children's children now enjoy
a childhood of a different kind
Less simple than it was back then,
but still of children's minds.

I hope in time when they recall
their years of long ago.
It's with love and joy and fondest thoughts,
as they watch their children grow.

But for me my time is almost o'er,
no dreams of future plans.
It's hard to have a dream come true,
when the ones you love are in a far-off land.

No one knows the hurt you feel,
when your world is torn apart.
No one can tell you the pain will ease,
when you have a broken heart.

You miss the hugs and kisses,
you miss the tears and sighs.
All you have are memories
that will cause a teary eye.

So as I watch the pure white shroud
settle o'er the trees and fields
It brings to mind a peaceful time,
of how a young heart feels.

A time locked in one's memory,
of childish pranks and schemes
when the hopes and fears of everyone,
were only down to dreams.

When soon this earthly coil's shook off,
and I know it is my time
Forget me not when you doth hear,
a sound far off of those softly tinkling wind chimes.

Number Five May Avenue

We lived in back to back two ups two downs
but as kids, where we lived we didn't care,
Not exactly the poshest part of town,
we could have lived just anywhere.

It mattered not what address you had,
no gardens to play in, just a street,
We had friends so it wasn't all bad,
not many cars or lorries for us to greet.

In fact, there was hardly any traffic all day,
so we could put down coats to make a goal.
There was plenty of room to run and play,
but it was hard on your skin playing football.

In the summer time we'd play out till late,
not really caring if we scraped a knee.
But getting hot and sweaty, and in quite a state,
It was so very good to feel that we were free.

Sometimes we'd play upon waste ground,
spaces created because of the war.
Where houses had been, but were now knocked down,
but the spaces we played on were rough and raw.

There was a lot of that sort of damage around our way,
Being but a baby I had no recall.
It must have been terrible back in the day
there were some who had lived through it all.

Being just kids we had no sense,
it only mattered that we were having fun.
With no way of knowing what it all meant
we didn't mean to upset anyone.

Playing games and going to school,
trying to keep our noses clean.
Sticking to, and following, all of the rules
was a lot harder than it may seem.

When the weather was bad it was harder still,
we couldn't help getting under mam's feet.
To keep behaving took all of our will,
glad when we were able to play in the street.

Odd times off to the park we'd go,
but most times to Rockford, a field beside a drain.
The park was a good three miles or so,
Rockford only two miles there and back again.

We'd play football there for most of the day,
most times the weather was quite fair.
As it grew late, homeward we'd wend our way,
but if the weather was bad, we didn't care.

If it started to rain, then we'd start to run,
sometimes the rain would come down in sheets
It didn't bother us much for we'd had so much fun,
sheltering under the bridge at the end of Woodhall Street.

Or under the bridges on Stoneferry Road,
between them at full tilt we'd run.
There were three of them all told,
getting wet though was all part of the fun.

RON STEELE

Home at last, I'll never forget,
after it had rained for two hours or so.
Mam would say, 'how did you get so wet?'
'It's been raining, didn't you know?'

Around the ear I'd receive a well-aimed clip,
sent to bed to dream of far-off lands.
With a sore ear I'd still get a good night's kip,
and dream of playing the flute in a marching band.

Which by the way, wasn't really so grand
years later having fun dressing up in boy scouts' uniform.
Playing a flute in a marching band,
and camping out many miles from home.

I was a member of the peewit patrol,
we messed about something cruel.
Being patrol leader, they did as they were told,
just kidding really, we had lots of laughs just playing the fool.

But there was a serious side too,
giving where we could help and aid.
Lots of good deeds in the community we'd do
but Sunday was best, on the church parade.

We'd gather outside St. Saviour's church hall,
when we were all present and correct
Stood in the freezing cold for our roll call,
then we'd march off, playing tunes that were very select.

Though I must say, without wishing to brag,
with drums, flutes and bugles that made quite a din.
The sound we made wasn't half bad,
playing tunes like 'When the saints go marching in.'

But sometimes the weather wasn't good for playing the flute
dressed in short-sleeved shirts and khaki shorts
Playing with numb fingers made it hard to toot,
with the wind whistling up places where it didn't ought.

We had loads of good times back then,
though hardships we mentally glossed over.
But I don't think I'd go back again,
of all those shortcomings I'm not a lover.

Going to the loo in the pouring rain,
only one tap, and that was outside.
A tap that would freeze up time and again,
out in our two-metre-square back yard.

For hot water we had a large kettle to boil,
and a gas-powered boiler from a valve on the wall.
On wash days with this mam would ease her toil,
which on looking back wasn't safe at all.

Just a tatty rubber pipe between us and disaster,
lots of things that were wrong back then that you did.
At the time I didn't think that it mattered,
you knew no better, you were only a kid.

As I grew up I would myself ask,
what would be going on inside my head.
What would become my future task?
Would I find a girl, a girl to wed?

In time I swopped play for work,
and most of my friends just drifted away.
No time left to play on Rockford or in the park,
but the really close friends would always stay.

RON STEELE

Every day of the week my apprenticeship filled,
until on October 24th 1963, a day that teared my eye
To stick at my apprenticeship, I had to be strong-willed,
for this was the day my father died.

On the day my father died,
lots of things to him I wanted to say.
For the first time in my life I really cried,
everything in an instant, just blown away.

He died of a massive heart attack,
he never said how ill he was.
For personal courage he never lacked
saying he was ill would be considered a bit of a wuss.

Four months later I met a girl,
so sadly she never met my pops.
This someone completely change my world,
I think they would have liked each other a lot.

A couple of years later I married that girl,
she bore our children with loving care.
She became the whole of my world,
sad to think that my pops wasn't there.

He would have loved grandchildren to sit on his knee,
giving them treats and singing to them old-time ditties.
It's sad that we will never see
that wonderful expression of love, more's the pity.

Then the houses had to go, a council decider,
after all they were very old and run down.
It was done to make the roads wider
and everyone moved to a better part of town

Strangely this effect didn't cause me much grief,
maybe because I had moved on with my life.
In progress I have always had a strong belief,
so my world was centred on my children and wife.

But each time I pass what's left of my street,
I feel somehow drawn to the past
Maybe because that I am incomplete,
but whatever the feeling, it's swift to pass

Perhaps I should have made a record,
about living in a house that was less than neat.
Perhaps we'll never regain that same accord
as we had in number 5 May Avenue, Bedford Street.

A declaration of love

A lifetime ago, or so it seems,
I met a girl, a girl of my dreams.
It's strange to think that since we met,
I have had not one hour, minute or second of regret.

When one is young, or really any age,
one wishes one could turn life's page
To see beyond the present time,
and catch a glimpse of a future that will be mine.

Life's journey is like an unfamiliar track
with twists and turns and no turning back.
No matter what road we take,
on the way we'll make mistakes.

You have always given anyone a helping hand,
and never lost faith in the things you've planned.
I know that with your undying love,
there's naught between me and heaven above.

Your kindness has always been the essence of our love,
shining as doth a light from up above.
never a bad dream or a time of regret,
could ever spoil the love I have for you, my darling Margaret.

A Frostways bus ride

On the corner of Cleveland and Chapman
stood our school, austere and tall
The girls on the first floor, the boys on the ground,
bordered on two sides by a wall.

Every year around the middle of summer,
we'd go on a Frostways bus ride
To the coast of North Yorkshire we'd travel,
to Scarborough, by the seaside.

Early in the year we'd start saving,
about two shillings a week
The teachers would map out a schedule,
saying when our savings should peak.

It was hard for some kids to manage,
even half of the money they'd want.
Not for one kid called Malcolm, well,
he always paid up front.

We'd all be up early that morning,
in the playground is where we would meet.
All the kids who had paid up their money,
which in our case was most of our street.

Most of the kids were in their Sunday best clothes,
except for Malcolm, who had very good gear
He would dress the same as always,
as he did throughout the whole of the year.

Grey flannel trews, creased down the front,
clean white shirt with pressed collar and cuffs
Made the rest of us look a little untidy,
but we didn't care if we looked like scruffs.

All lined up in our class teams,
ready to board the bus, whose driver was Mick
Waiting for all the late comers,
when they arrived we gave them some stick.

Our teams were red, blue, green and yellow,
each colour alphabetically picked
If you had a name at the end of the alphabet,
you'd be in yellow team and have the rest of the class licked.

We had the best team, which was yellows
best in football, cricket and track
Only the older kids could beat us,
fighting spirit we never lacked.

The assistant head teacher, called Towers,
blew his whistle to board the bus
As we filed on board, I thought it quite strange
That Towers was smaller than us.

RON STEELE

Eventually the buses started moving,
we all settled noisily in to our seats.
Travelling which for us was such a great distance,
It really was quite a treat.

We set off northwards up Stoneferry Road,
passing the end of our street
As we turned into West Carr Lane,
we stopped, Kenny Wilkinson to meet.

It seemed silly not to pick him up there,
for his house was on the way out.
It saved him a long trek to school,
for nothing, there was no doubt.

Our teacher soon shouted, be quiet!
For we were quite noisy, it's true.
The noise quickly hushed to a bearable hum,
except for the seniors at the back, of which there were quite a few.

Poshly-dressed Malcolm would brag about going
To Scarborough many times in the past
About always going by train,
and how he always got there so fast.

But we didn't mind, it was all so new to us,
most of us didn't go so very far
I was lucky I got to go Withernsea, sometimes by train,
on a Sunday there and back with my sis, Ma and Pa.

Having said that I still enjoyed our trip out on the bus
stopping off in Thornton-le-Dale for the toilet and ice cream.
In the early fifties it was a very quiet little village,
thinking back, it was more like a dream.

A DIVERSITY OF VERSE

We'd pull up at the ice cream shop by the side of a stream,
using some of our spending money for sweets and some pop.
Finishing our ice creams, we got back on the bus,
and settled noisily down for the next stop.

The next stop was to eat our packed lunches,
I had ham sandwiches and a flask of tea.
By the time I got to drink it, the tea was quite stewed,
but it was wet and warm and that would do for me.

Perched on the top of Sutton Bank we'd have our 'eats',
on a nice clear day, you could see across the hills and dales
Watching the gliders silently soaring,
with bright coloured wings like ship's sails.

Back on the bus off to Scarborough, we got there not long after lunch,
the sea was calm in the bay, hardly a ripple to be seen
The donkeys were standing doing nothing,
there was no one to ride them, it seemed.

We were left by our teachers to our own devices,
people would have a fit these days, and create a bit of a fuss.
To think that we had no supervision,
just given a time to get back to the bus.

So me and my friends went shopping first,
thinking some trinkets to buy
Something for mum as a memento,
that was cheap and that caught my eye.

We'd buy figurines made of chalk,
painted with bright colours of gloss.
There were dogs, cats, budgies and allsorts,
which was the best to buy, we were at a loss.

Eventually we'd settle on something
carefully wrapped and secure
Then it was off to the sweet shop,
to buy something tasty, for sure.

The amusements were next on the list,
to try and win a keepsake for us.
But, after hours of feverishly trying,
it was time to get back to the bus.

It wasn't always good weather,
sometimes the rain would fall
But we didn't really mind about that,
because usually a good time was had by all.

Back on the bus warm and dry,
we headed out and for home.
With everyone checked and accounted for,
we left no one lost and alone.

It was late in the day when we set off back,
once again settling noisily down
Talking about what we'd done and bought
heading back to our home town.

When we arrived home it was already dark,
the long summer nights seemed to be gone
Our house was only a short walk from school,
so to get home didn't take long.

My mum was always pleased with whatever I brought her,
there didn't seem anything for my pops I could buy
Only expensive items, beyond my purse,
I'll wait while Christmas and buy him a tie.

Malcolm never showed us what he had bought,
in a carrier bag he always kept wrapped
He always bragged about everything else,
he was embarrassed, perhaps.

Never mattered to us when we were kids,
who had what, and how much.
We didn't care because we always had fun,
which I think was a very nice touch.

A seasonal tale

Trees stand stark at break of day,
from a night that's long to end
They groan to greet the morning sun,
when icy winds their branches bend.

By day the sun's an eerie light
as from a candle glow
But soon those winds like wolves will howl,
and turn the winter rain to snow.

Silent falls the pure white shroud,
all over hill and dale
A time when life's exceeding slow,
and winter's sunshine's pale.

Sharp winds that give a watery eye,
loud footfalls on the frozen snow,
shadowy forms with collars raised,
wearily trudging, homeward go.

A welcome lantern from a window beams,
as moonlight glistens upon the snow
There's heard the singing of seasonal rhymes,
of remembered yuletides long ago.

Beside the fire burning bright
warming the chill from one's old bones.
With the door firmly closed against the cold,
one's safe and sound within one's home.

Stars like diamonds on black velvet shine
against the cold night sky
Clouds across a silvery moon
silently float by.

But soon the long winter's night is o'er,
the wind bestills its painful moan
When we will look upon the break of day,
and greet a brand new dawn.

A winter's tale

This time of year that Americans call fall,
the sun we see through a pale saffron veil.
The trees so stark with leaves stripped bare,
this gloomy start of a winter's tale.

Scattered leaves heaped upon the ground,
weave a carpet of mottled colours, a pretty sight.
Rook's nests seen in trees black and tall,
with echoing caws in a heady flight.

Rooks with wings as black as jet
glide stark against grey skies above my head.
Chilling winds around runny noses,
and chattering teeth with words unsaid.

Tear filled eyes welling to a flood,
Hands that are swollen chapped and raw,
holy wellies that are of no use
thin frail kids frozen to the core.

Autumn passes and the wind blows cold
grey clouds gather over vale and hill.
Every creature heads for its home,
only stark tall trees left to face the night's chill.

Then silent fall the flakes of snow,
leave prints where feet have trodden down.
More snow to cover where feet have been,
paint the cold, stark beauty of a winter's crown.

Pale saffron sun, late in the day,
a rising wind gathers up the clouds.
The stars twinkle softly in the cold night sky.
as the moon is covered by a ghostly shroud.

Winds stir up flurries of purest white,
and unearthly moans from things unseen.
Dark clouds part and the stars shine through,
casting an eerie light on a frosty scene.

Glistening snow like diamonds shine,
the wind has died to barely a sigh.
All is still in the cold night air,
when an owl on the wing floats silently by.

She hunts for the creature that braves the night,
hoping to feed to dispel the cold.
Will she be able to find a meal?
the only chance of growing old.

Soon the long night will at last be o'er,
as we await the sun's meagre heat.
It brings the weakest of smiles to an old man's face,
hard to smile with frozen hands and feet.

Children playing winter games on icy paths and frozen ponds
seeming not to notice the cold and damp.
Playing without a care in the world,
until they get hot ache and cramp.

Then it's off home to a fireside, cosy and warm,
with hot drinks and embers bright.
Maybe tomorrow we'll do it all again,
but mum says that's enough for tonight.

The days become longer as we head towards spring,
the sun becomes warmer, longer and higher in the sky.
The wind has less of a bite
to cause a teary eye.

Winter soon will be but a mere memory,
dark grey skies give way to azure blue.
Leafless trees begin to bloom,
and the world once again will have a pleasing hue.

Always believe in angels

Always believe in angels no matter how difficult life may be,
along life's road the end is sometimes hard to see.
But if you believe, you can survive the sternest of life's tests,
for inner strength brings inner pride, to someone at their very best.

You never know what may be around any corner on any day,
but if you believe, there'll always be a light to guide your way.
Belief is hardest to maintain when the whole world says you're wrong,
so never doubt your self-belief, it's your way of staying strong.

Believing in angels in itself is not the way to end your woes,
but it can be the strength you need to take on all your foes.
Whether or not angels do exist is for each of us to decide,
but the fact still remains, from the world we cannot hide.

If you believe, you'll never be in the dark or on your own,
faith will always bring you peace of mind, and always bless your home.
Remember when you're down at heart, and you have no one to tell,
he'll always have a friendly ear, your light, your guide, Matt, your angel.

to Paula, with love from Dad

Anniversary

The years go by and we notice not,
but at times we note one passing.
We do not have to count those years,
when our love is everlasting.

To be as one needs constant care,
to make our mark upon life's page.
To be in love's for everyone,
no matter what your age.

Our hopes and dreams when we set out,
upon this journey long
Make in our hearts a certainty,
when we know our love is strong.

From each to the other we give a piece
of our own body and soul.
Sure in our hearts that it's kept safe,
whilst we are growing old.

Upon life's road the burden's shared,
all troubles and tasks are halved.
Knowing for sure we'll reach the end,
although that road be hard.

When your whole world is the light,
that's in another's eyes
Then your whole world is in the sound
of that same person's sighs.

When we want someone to hold our hand,
being down and in need of a friend
The one we love will be right there,
on that we can depend.

The pain inside when we're apart,
and that loved one's arms are missed
Is soon dispelled and blown away,
just by that loved one's kiss.

Value is of no concern,
from earth to heaven above.
There is no way to gauge its worth,
this priceless thing called love.

So even after all these years,
our love will always be.
Strong and steadfast as a rock,
through each anniversary.

All my love, Ron

Bygones

Years ago when life was slow,
and I but a child with nowhere to go
Many a dream I had back then,
of what the future would bring, and when.

The thoughts of a child are simple and plain,
no dreams of success or financial gain,
But instead, a wondering of what I'd be,
When all the decisions came down to me.

Between those dreams I didn't care
whether my life was good, bad or fair.
Hot dusty summers with holes in my shoes,
cold damp winters, with leaky wellies too.

It didn't matter what I had back there,
because the means of my friends were just as bare.
You cannot be jealous of another's lot.
if all he has is what you've got.

Sitting on the kerb beside a cobbled street,
playing with the tar that's like a sticky sweet.
Long hot school hols with time on our hands,
in days back then we could roam the land.

Not many cars around our way,
the roads were quiet most of the day
Only when factory folk headed for home,
were the roads too busy for a child alone.

Our parents had not the fears of parents today,
children were safer then, in many ways.
They let us roam the streets at will,
surer then than now that we'd come to no ill.

With friends I'd meet, and stay out till dark,
football in the street, or down at the park.
Old fashioned boots, sporting old leather studs,
we'd sling round our necks, and be off to Rockford.

Rockford was a field beside a drain,
two miles from my home and back again.
With coats put down to make a goal,
there'd be hours of fun with an old leather ball.

When tired we'd lie down, and rest in the grass,
until all too soon the day had passed
With two miles to home we'd wend our way,
if it stays fine we'll be back another day.

The weather was not always so dry,
sometimes there'd be rain from a dark grey sky.
Whilst watching the raindrops make rings in the pools,
I'd remember that soon we'd be back at school.

When that morning comes, and the halls are gone,
they won't be much to speak of, except by one.
He's the boy who had more than the rest,
who looked like his togs were his Sunday best.

Malcolm's his name, but he's not like us,
he went to the seaside on a Frostways bus.
At the seaside for a fortnight he always stayed,
we'd go sometimes, but just for the day.

He told of beaches with nobody there,
two weeks of breathing clean fresh air.
One day for us there was just the same,
because we got to go on an old steam train.

With hair combed flat and grey flannel trews,
clean white shirt and mended shoes.
Checking the times of all the trains,
from Wilmington to Withernsea and back again.

I'd run back home in breathless glee,
with the next train's time to Withernsea.
At Wilmington, our station, in the ticket office hall,
we'd buy our tickets at a hole in the wall.

When my dad paid the money we'd climb the stair,
for our station's platform was up in the air.
High on an embankment some forty feet,
it seemed miles above old Foster Street.

While we'd wait for the train, my dad would chat
to a man across the lines, in a dusty flat cap.
We'd see this man almost each time we went,
he worked where my dad worked, at Earle's cement.

The train would arrive, and off we'd go,
looking down from the windows at the scene below.
Over the bridge above Stoneferry road,
then noisily passing close to my home.

Racing through crossings with big white gates,
I'd wave to the traffic that would patiently wait.
Stopping at stations that have now sadly gone,
stations with names, some short, and some long.

At Southcoates, Marfleet, and Hedon too,
lots of people got on, but sometimes only a few.
Ryehill and Burstwick the next station's nameplate,
with colourful flowers, and a man on the gate.

Passing factories, goods yards, houses, then fields,
with the continuous sound of steel upon steel
Keyingham, Ottringham, Patrington's last,
this magical journey's gone by so fast.

Then in the distance the lighthouse is seen,
against the blue sky, standing tall white and clean.
Scarcely before the train's come to a halt,
I'd open the door and from it I'd vault.

Running headlong to the station's main gate,
to get on to the sand I could hardly wait
Impatiently I'd queue my tickets to show,
surely the man knows I've been here before.

I'd dash onto the sand without any care,
whilst my dad paid a man for two deckchairs.
In bare feet across pebbles I'd painfully step,
gingerly walking to get my feet wet.

Cold and rough was this great North Sea,
its colour brown, like a cup of cold tea.
At midday we'd go and get something to eat,
sometimes in a café for a fish and chip treat.

After our meal to the amusements we'd go,
to play the machines, whilst mum and dad played bingo.
My dad nearly always, well most times he won,
but, when he didn't, he still had fun.

One whole afternoon he won nothing at all,
but on leaving the man gave him the pick of the stall.
The day's almost over and, we're off back to the train,
maybe another fine Sunday, we'll come here again.

Dedicated to my late father, who worked so hard in twelve hour shifts of overtime, to provide for my sister and myself. God bless you Pops.

Children

Oh what joy when your children are born,
their smiles and laughter make a house a home.
You're filled with pride when they face the world
it matters not whether they're boys or girls.

No matter their age you worry and fret,
but all the pain and joy you never forget.
In every way, your child is the best,
in every way standing out from the rest.

No matter their faults you'll always forgive,
and though you may guide, it's their life to live.
With worry and doubt you let them go their own way,
and hope they'll do better than you in your day.

You're proud of them in every way,
there's always pride throughout their days.
Then, once again a child is born,
a child to make a house a home.

A smiling face that's full of fun,
a beautiful granddaughter or grandson
a beautiful face that's meek and mild,
the smiling face of our grandchild.

Dreamy

I sit and watch a meandering stream,
and in my mind I chance to dream
Of dragons wild and damsels fair,
bold knights and castles in the air.

As the sunlight glistens on this peaceful flow,
a breeze sways the long grass to and fro.
On a summer's day with little to do,
watching cotton bud clouds sail by on azure blue.

A fish swims by in the waters clear,
the sun warms my back, and it's peaceful here.
A lark on high sings a shrill note,
it knows the summer will be only too short.

I close my eyes and dream a dream,
of far-off lands, mountains and streams.
Of a midnight sun and northern lights,
of desert sands, and Arabian nights.

Jungles deep, full of animals wild,
a Christmas tree, and gifts for a child.
Angelic voices from a church on a hill,
a peal of bells on a night so still.

But my dream is spoiled by a distant sound,
I awake with dark clouds all around.
Spots of rain splash upon my face,
I head for shelter, and find a place.

Across the field stands an old wooden barn,
inside it's dry, nice and warm.
On a pile of hay, I peep through the door,
watching the rain as it begins to pour.

A lightning flash from dark angry clouds,
thunder rumbles long and loud,
A strong wind rises stirring the trees,
no time for flying for birds and bees.

In a little while the storm passes by,
the sun comes out for the world to dry.
All the dark clouds roll away,
and once again it's a nice summer's day.

As the sun shines bright on this peaceful scene,
against the distant clouds a rainbow's seen
One of green, blue, yellow, and red,
but the setting sun says it's time for bed.

Off to bed to perhaps dream again,
of summer sun, and summer rain.
Who knows where one's dreams might fly,
with cotton bud clouds on an azure sky.

with love from Grandma & Grandpops XXX

Friends

In memory of a lovely lady and dear friend, Audrey Brown

No one can know just how you feel,
or gauge your depth of pain.
But as friends, we know in time,
you'll wear a smile again.

We cannot cure the hurt inside,
when one so dear departs.
No spoken word, or gesture made,
can heal a broken heart.

But the ache inside, in time will ease,
with courage that you'll find.
Having the strength to carry on,
will bring you peace of mind.

As each day dawns, you'll not forget,
remembrance will bring a little tear.
Memories of more joyful days,
will stay in your mind so clear.

There is no way to fill the void,
or ever replace the past.
But there'll always be a shoulder here,
with a friendship made to last.

With love to Mick from Margaret and Ron.

God, a perception of

Since the dawn of time, there has been a god, good or bad.
A deity that could explain the natural phenomena back then,
Praying for salvation, a lifeline of hope was all they had.
from the very outset the who, why and where was down to him.

In 1095 Pope Urban II instigated the first Crusade,
to free the 'holy land' of non-believing Muslims.
It seems very strange that a religion that would the world persuade,
that it was all peace and love, and forgiving mankind for all his sins

Who could wage a bloody war in this deities' name,
rape, pillage, and commit innumerable and despicable sinful acts?
And all the while reasoning with an excuse so lame,
as to believe that they were justified, to do what they did 'in his name.'

Until man teaches his children to treat others with respect,
having a different view from their own that's neither bad nor incorrect
The world will struggle for its peace; but I believe a time will come,
when there will be peace for everyone.

Actions in defence of their so-called 'one true god'
can only make the task harder to make good.
One can only hope that sooner or later there will be
a saviour of the world in the name of one or another deity.

Kids

Kids with grubby faces
and sweet angelic eyes
never dream of far-off places,
whilst playing with mud pies.

They never notice time is passing,
or whether it's hot or cold,
They never wonder if what they're doing
is the thing that they've been told.

They never stop and worry
that mum would have a fit,
if she should find them digging
at the bottom of the old sand pit.

They never change into play clothes
to save the wear and tear,
they're much too keen on having fun,
it's not that they don't care.

They never believe it's time for bed,
they suspect an adult con
the playing time's gone by so fast,
the day never is too long.

So when they're scrubbed clean,
and tucked up in their bed,
and they fall fast asleep,
whilst the story book is read

Don't grumble about the cleaning
and the washing that's all in a pile,
just think of all those blessings,
and you'll always rise a smile.

Thinking back upon those days
when you did what you did,
you weren't always an angel,
but you were always a kid.

Leslie

My friend Leslie, of Keighley born,
strong of will though frail of form
Strong of mind though poor of health,
wisdom in truth his greatest wealth.
With his roots firmly set but his spirit free,
of Keighley born was my friend Leslie.

Oft times stubborn, but a principled man,
He would answer a call with a helping hand.
Simplicity for him in all his tastes,
though simple his life, it was never a waste.
A family man, plain for all to see,
of Keighley born was my friend Leslie.

A cheery greeting whenever we came,
on leaving a plea, to come again.
Our visits so short with this colourful man,
who had all the charm of Bronte land.
He'll forever stay in our memory,
of Keighley born was my friend Leslie.

Dedicated to the memory of my wife's uncle and my friend, Leslie Mitchell

Lonesome

Wandering aimless, lost and alone,
the rain-soaked streets of a sleeping city
Only the echoing of footsteps that are my own,
disturbs a night of little pity.

The cold wind rises and starts to moan,
it gnaws with fury at my heart and soul.
Nowhere is there a place to call home,
or in someone's arms I can enfold.

Memories from the dark recesses of my mind,
faded images in a golden hue.
The clarity that I'll never again find,
has gone like my youth, before I knew.

Lights from windows as I pass quietly by
reflect on the hard wet flagstones.
Above the wind's howl is heard a baby cry,
that is silenced with love from the heart of a home.

Loneliness can be in the heart or the mind,
in a crowded street or a desert wasteland.
A soul needs someone who's tender and kind,
who'll dispel one's fears with a tender hand.

The black sky of night fades swiftly away,
lights go out on cold wet streets.
The dawn is breaking, it's another day,
and I'm still standing on my own two feet.

When will we begin to understand
and treat each one as they deserve?
Offering to all a helping hand,
and then quality of life we'll help to preserve.

Love

Love could be anything you want it to be.
Love could be the earth, the sky, the sea.
Love could be the sharing of all things dear
Love could be the voice you long to hear.

Love could be the tear on your child's face
Love could be the smile with which it's replaced.
Love could be the heart that's warm and true.
Love could be the eyes of purest blue.

Love could be the things you never forget
But love to me is you, Margaret.
Love was absent in my life,
until you became my wife.

Then love overflowed in my world,
with the birth of our baby girl
Overflowing once more with joy,
upon the birth of our baby boy.

Through the years our children have reflected your love,
before, beyond, and all else above.
Their joy, your joy, their pain, your pain,
yours was the smile they saw time and again.

Now, years on, there is a new joy to share,
a grandchild is sent to our love and care.
It matters not if it's a boy or girl,
It's the most precious gift in all the world.

When our time is past and we are old,
and all the stories to our grandchildren told
Our love will be, as it's always been,
ever true, ever sure, evergreen.

All my love, Ron.

Love's Dedication
To Margaret with love

As the sun rises through the morning mist,
autumn begins its new colour page.
The dewy grass is as yet un kissed,
by the sun's pale saffron rays.

And as your dark brown hair doth match the leaves,
and your blue eyes the deep sparkling pools.
You bring to mind a wistful summers breeze.
so I feel not this autumn wind so cool.

Through all these years you have been my rock,
my strength against life's storm.
Yours was the love that kept me whole,
and made our house a home.

RON STEELE

An angelic face without a frown,
soft tender hands that are so warm.
A touch as light as feathery down,
and a smile that's all your own

Those blue smiling eyes that melt my soul,
did steal my heart away.
A precious jewel without a crown,
that shines as doth a sunny day.

But unlike the flower whose gorgeous bloom,
that must one day fade and die.
Your beauty will stay forever fresh,
in this beholder's eye.

When the path I tread as yet grows dark,
I know that heaven's morning's come,
your spirit will fill my heart,
and I'll know my race is run.

It will guide and guard me through eternity,
forever by my side.
For so it has been for all to see,
since you became my bride.

When that shining light that is your spirit,
is heaven bound and free
There'll always remain a spark on earth,
through all eternity.

And when your soul and mine entwine,
on that great and wondrous plain
That event will be earth's sad loss,
and heaven's eternal gain.

All my love, Ron.

My reason to be
(Lyrics for a song)

Here comes the morning sun,
there goes another night without you.
So many things I should have said and done,
why did I ever doubt you?
Watching the stars just fade away
like all our dreams and plans,
now there's only one set of footprints
wandering across the sand.

(Chorus)
You were my world, you were my reason to be,
even though you were unkind
You still made the best of me.
It keeps going through my mind,
that I'll never forget, you were my reason to be.

I'm just sitting by the railroad track,
listening to that lonesome whistle blow
wondering if you'll ever come back,
wondering if you'll ever know
How much I really loved you,
how much I really cared and didn't show.
even though you were untrue.
Why did you have to go?

(Chorus)
You were my world, you were my reason to be,
even though you were unkind
You still made the best of me,
It keeps going through my mind
that I'll never forget, you were my reason to be.

Seagulls glide on high as I sit here on my own,
the wind murmurs your name, as I recall your eyes.
they are as blue as the skies of home.
As I heave a heavy lonesome sigh
I gaze across an empty beach,
praying to the gods on high,
that your love is not out of reach.

(Chorus)
You were my world, you were my reason to be,
even though you were unkind
You still made the best of me.
It keeps going through my mind,
that I'll never forget, you were my reason to be,
my reason to be.

My Mum, Olive

As I held you in my arms, we talked of days gone by,
of family, and friends we've known, and joyful tears we've cried.
You tried to tell me how you felt, though the words you couldn't form
I seemed to know just what you meant, with an understanding all our own.

You tried to say you'd done your best, all through my early years,
to be a kind and loving mum, kissing away my fears.
I tried to tell you of the love each day I felt for you,
like yours, a love that's from the heart, one that's pure and true.

Through all the years you were infirm your spirit was always free,
loved by the ones that cared for you, was plain for all to see.
A complaint or moan was never heard from this lady meek and mild,
so sweet was she that nurses cared for her as though she were a child.

Your life when lived was full of love, you gave your heart and soul,
no malicious thought or evil deed was ever yours at all.
You clung to life so valiantly, but, in the end your fight was lost,
then quietly you slipped away, so peacefully at last.

Your time with us is over now, your time on earth is o'er,
your soul on wings is heaven bound to dwell forever more.
At each day's end I lay me down, knowing you are at rest,
I go to sleep knowing you're there, whispering 'good night, God bless'.

Written with love for and on behalf of my darling wife Margaret, whose love for her mother Olive knew no bounds.

My Wife

Written for and on behalf of my darling wife Margaret

A lifetime ago, or so it seems,
I met a girl, a girl of my dreams.
It's strange to think that since we met,
there has not been one day, hour or minute of regret.

When one is young, or any age,
one often wishes to turn life's page
To see beyond the present time,
to glimpse the future that will be mine.

Life's journey is like an unfamiliar track,
with twists and turns, but no turning back.
We get one choice of the road we take,
and along that road, mistakes we make.

But with someone like you to hold my hand,
I've never lost faith in the things we've planned.
I know that with your undying love,
there's naught between you and heaven above.

I look back on the past that was my life
and marvel at the girl who became my wife.
Through thick and thin to our journey's end,
not just a wife, but my best friend.

All my love, Ron.

Olive #2

What is an angel, does anyone know?
recognised good deeds, or a bit of a show.
No fame or reward for the likes of you and me.
but unsung heroes there'll always be,

No reward for the decent women and men,
nothing for those who laboured back then.
Women like Olive who, throughout her life,
who was never far away from its trouble and strife.

She toiled for her own, and helped other folk,
her heart became tired but, it never broke.
Always remaining steadfast, loyal, and true,
the frustrations she felt were never on view.

Her generation less open but honest within,
more fearful and watchful of committing a sin.
But from her background and status in life,
women were expected to become a man's wife.

In that era society was constricted by class,
which was hard on a poor working lass.
I wonder if she was ever asked what she'd like to be,
or ever given a choice that was free.

Perhaps wanting no more than the path she had trod,
with unquestioning faith in her family and God.
I'll never know what years ago she felt,
of the loves in her life, or in the world in which she dwelt.

RON STEELE

Never knowing because, in life's cruellest fate,
she was robbed of the power to communicate
Illness left her in a frail empty shell,
the feelings she had, no one could tell.

From herself I feel, there would be no complaint,
just acceptance of her lot, this cruel slice of fate.
During her life, through tears of sadness and joy,
she raised with tender loving care a girl and a boy.

For myself, I am thankful for the daughter she bore,
for she's now my wife, and Olive my mother-in-law.
Wherever you go, or wherever you live,
you may meet an angel. That will be Olive.

From one who was privileged to be your son-in-law, Ron

That night

This story in verse is dedicated to my darling wife Margaret, without whose support and encouragement it would not have been written.

Angry clouds on a winter's night,
no stars to see, no moon shine bright.
Howling winds around chimneys tall,
cold wet streets where the rain doth fall.

Footsteps scrape across old cobble stones,
Worn-out shoes bring a chill to one's bones
The slow weary trudge of a figure alone,
on a dark stormy night, as he heads for home.

On a corner he stands, for a moment or so,
beneath a street lamp in its soft yellow glow
He stops to listen, but gone is the sound,
the howling wind no longer around.

He holds his breath, and with an ear he strains,
but all is still, save for the fall of the rain.
Nothing is moving on this cold damp night,
it's a time when the bravest souls take flight.

Someone stands there, across the street,
in a pool of light which shows two wet feet
No form can be seen above the knee,
no way of telling who it might be.

A whistle sounds, at a distance far,
distracts his eye for a moment there.
His gaze returns to across the street,
no more the sight of those two wet feet.

RON STEELE

No sound of footsteps hurrying away,
Was someone there? He could not say,
Maybe the night's playing tricks with his mind,
as he feels a chill of an unnatural kind.

His shoulders he shrugs beneath a wet coat,
a muffler he tightens around a dry throat.
Feeling that he, is once more alone,
continues his weary trudge toward home.

He pays no heed to the drip of the rain,
for the cold makes a numbness deep in his brain
He once again stops in a street lamp's glow,
his mind says run, but his feet won't go.

Something is there in the shadows so deep,
something is there that makes his flesh creep.
No sound except the splash of water down drains,
naught but the sound of the miserable rain.

With his collar erect, he turns once more,
when there comes a creak from a dark shop door.
The door swings open, with no hand to push,
the hairs on his neck stand up at a rush.

The coldness he felt because of the wet
is now colder by far, because of his sweat
Like a river of ice, it runs over his skin
at the thought in his mind, of what lies within.

He's drawn forward, as if by a force unknown,
to face something evil, in the darkness alone.
He steps through the portal that's dirty and grim,
shaking with fear at what lies within.

A DIVERSITY OF VERSE

With a straining eye, he searches the gloom,
but only shelves full of dust, in this old shop's room.
A feeble thought ran through his brain,
at least it's dry, and out of the rain,

He shuffles forward into the gloom,
over the threshold of this old shop's room.
The glow from the street lamp barely reaches inside,
a place full of shadows where evil might hide.

As he steps forward, the door creaks to a close,
he can do nothing to stop it, just as if he froze
All he could do was to stand and stare,
alone in the darkness, or was something else there?

There was not a sound in this old shop's room,
silent and dark as if in a tomb.
Trying to control the rate of his breath,
through his mind were racing thoughts of death.

Was he alone in the darkness standing there?
pale, statuesque and transfixed he stared.
Then from the shadows across the room,
came an eerie glow that pierced the gloom.

As enlargement made clear this evil sight,
like an animal's eyes that shine in the night
Two small orbs of the deepest red,
growing in size but without a head.

Closer and closer to his face they came,
oh how he wished he'd stayed out in the rain.
His feet from this spot he could not wrench,
as to his nostrils there came an evil stench.

He felt on his face the tears of a child,
and the hot moist breath of an animal wild.
Then with a sound like a hurricane's roar,
there came a swirling wind rising up from the floor.

With dust and debris flying all around,
it was hard to keep his feet on the ground.
It was not the fear that averted his stare,
but the clouds of dust that now filled the air.

Coughing and choking with eyes closed tight,
wondering if he would live through this night.
Then suddenly, the room was still again,
no sound at all, save that of the rain.

Strange, the rain's sound was not heard before,
for all was quiet, behind the old shop's door
But as he forced his eyes stark wide,
he could see through the door to the street outside.

Once more not a sound from the old shop's room,
the street light barely breaching its eerie gloom.
With feet of lead he trudged to the door,
anxious to be out in the rain once more.

As he dragged himself across the threshold again,
he felt on his face, the cool splash of the rain.
Once more came the feeling of being alone,
no idea of the time, he trudged towards home.

Something was strange on this already strange night,
he could not place this thing not right
But as he glazed up to a starless sky,
why should the street light catch his eye?

With its soft yellow glow, and its mantle of gas,
but how much time on that night had passed?
For the yellow glow was no longer soft,
an electric light bulb was now up aloft.

With his mind trying to make some reason or rhyme,
on the night air came a church clock's chime.
Not keeping count, he was not sure,
if the clock had struck five, six, or more.

With a shrug of his shoulders he wended his way,
too tired to care if it were night or day.
None of this was real, or so it seemed,
perhaps it was all, just the worst of a dream.

On his way, a shop window he chanced to pass,
and there his reflection he saw in the glass.
The man standing there all bedraggled and wet,
surely that man was not him? But yet

This form was familiar, this one standing there,
but this man was old, and had silvery hair.
Was this real, or, maybe a dream?
he prayed that this was not some devilish scheme.

Mirrored it seemed in another era or time,
he wondered if he was going out of his mind.
Then, glancing along at the building next door,
on a board, a date he'd not seen before.

This date that he saw, he felt must be wrong,
in a decade he knew that he did not belong.
In a few moments he'd lost thirty years of his life,
in a panic his thoughts quickly turned to his wife.

What would she think when he did not come home?
what would she feel being left all alone?
If he looked like this now, with silvery hair,
what had time done to her and that skin so fair?

Hurrying along thinking the hour must be late,
in a short while he stood at his own garden gate.
As he waited there, on came the porch light,
an elderly lady put out the cat for the night.

This woman had once had a beauteous form,
but now she was stooping, weary and worn.
Whilst standing there she looked up and down,
this street from which there came not a sound.

How could she not see him standing there?
a mere ten feet from her aged stare.
He called out her name and waved a hand,
sadly, turning, the door behind her she slammed.

Standing alone, he pondered his fate,
then slowly and quietly, pushed open the gate.
Not daring to knock, through the window he peeped,
of this small terraced house, in a small quiet street.

In a dimly-lit room by a firelight's glow,
the old lady sat, her hair white as snow,
With a shawl around her shoulders wrapped,
and some bright coloured knitting there in her lap.

He thought as he stared at this tired old form,
how sad she looked sitting there all alone.
What should he do, where should he go?
perhaps the answer lies through that old shop door.

Back quickly he went through his own front gate,
back to the shop, where he might settle his fate,
Hurrying along those cold damp streets,
trembling with fear at what he might meet.

Turning the corner where the old shop lay,
in the sky a light, it was breaking day.
As he reached the spot, he caught his breath,
the shop was gone, there was nothing left.

All that was there was a burnt-out shell,
in this place where he'd been face to face with hell.
The old shop door's frame still stood,
like a silent gravestone of black charred wood.

As he stood there in silence trying to clear his brain,
the dawn was breaking, and gone was the rain.
In the doorway he saw a huddled form,
in ragged clothes on this cold damp morn.

A man it seemed of advancing years,
a heavy lined face, and eyes full of tears
With his collar turned up against his silvery hair,
in horror he saw, it was himself huddled there.

As he stood there unmoving, the man raised his eyes,
and from an unshaven face gave him a smile.
In a deep gravel voice, he heard the man say,
'I bet you are wondering how you got this way.

You won't find the answer at the bottom of a glass,
turn your life, before your future becomes your past.'
With a teary eye he looked up and saw,
a mantle, glowing, as it had before.

The old shop itself, no longer dirty and grim,
but a cheerful light, shone out from within.
No huddled form in the shop door lay,
the old man was gone, it was late in the day.

All he knew was, he had to go home,
to his dear sweet wife sitting there all alone.
Hot, breathless and wet, he reached his front gate,
catching his breath, he dared to wait.

But just as he did, on came the porch light,
and a beautiful woman put out the cat for the night.
As their eyes met his heart lost its fear,
as down that beautiful face, there trickled a tear.

Through the open gate and up the path he raced,
And their bodies entwined in a loving embrace.
He didn't know what had happened to change his life.
all he knew, he was safe now, in the arms of his wife.

The mirror

In the mirror I look and see,
these eyes that are looking back at me
eyes that were once as bright as day,
eyes that are now cloudy and grey.
In the autumn of my life I stand and stare,
oh where is that boy of yesteryear?

The mirror, like the camera, cannot lie,
but we see with the mind and not with the eye.
So many years have flown by so fast,
and in the mirror reflections of all the scars of the past.
This face that has felt many a smile and many a tear,
oh where is that boy of yesteryear?

Feelings that the mirror cannot see,
are held inside, but long to be free.
Freedom to do the things of one's youth,
things that you cannot, without facing the truth.
Once things one would do without turning a hair,
oh where is that boy of yesteryear?

In the mirror you watch your children grow,
and then they have children before you know.
As a child or a youth time would never seem to pass,
but in the mirror's reflection it's flown by so fast.
You still have the love of the one held so dear,
oh where is that boy of yesteryear?

In the mirror you see the world quickly change,
whether for better or worse, you can't rearrange.
Each one must do the best that he can,
trying to build his life to a plan.
But, if the plan goes astray, no one will care,
oh where is that boy of yesteryear?

The mirror's reflection will soon grow dim,
except for the memories one holds within.
The passing of time can do damage untold,
but with strength of mind one will never grow old.
At the end of one's time, all things are made clear,
I am that boy of yesteryear.

The Toad

My country cottage was small and neat,
and set at the end of a village street.
One morning in May, outside my front door,
I saw a sight I'd not seen before.

There, in broad daylight, fat and green,
was the largest toad I'd ever seen
Round and fat in the middle of the road,
with a smug expression, sat a large green toad.

Upon his head was a small gold crown,
with glistening jewels all around
Wearing a pair of silver shoes,
and reading a copy of the morning news.

I thought I was dreaming, but it was not night,
as I gazed in awe at this comical sight.
Oh what a shock when I heard him talk,
for words came out, instead of a croak!

He bid me 'good day' whilst reading the news,
and upon the weather, he asked me my views.
'Don't you think it's a beautiful sky?'
Quite taken aback, I did not reply.

I sat down at the road side completely amazed,
in silent awe I just simply gazed.
Did this creature really talk?
Clearly, in words, instead of a croak.

Once again he asked me my views,
upon various things that appeared in the news.
'I really don't know,' I finally said.
This morning's paper, I had, as yet, not read.

Lowering his paper, he began to smile,
staring at me for quite a while.
'I used to be like you,' he said.
'A normal person, and very well read.'

'Oh really,' I answered. Which seemed impolite,
to suggest his remarks were not quite right.
I could not believe I was hearing these sounds,
from a bright green toad that was fat and round.

He appeared not to mind that I doubted his word,
even though a talking toad seemed quite absurd,
And that I should be sat in the middle of the road,
actually conversing with a fat green toad.

Very well mannered, and with a cultured voice,
he did not shout or create a noise
But instead carried on quietly reading the morning news,
patiently waiting for me to air my views.

After what seemed an hour of thinking what to say,
finally, stupidly, I remarked, 'Fine weather today.'
He nodded and smiled, quite kindly I thought,
so, should I say more? Perhaps I ought.

What does one say to a fat green toad,
sat outside one's house in the middle of the road?
Does one converse on current affairs,
or does one discuss the market shares?

Talk of the world's fashion trends,
or simply gossip about odds and ends?
Maybe a particular sport might be apt
maybe about who for England should be capped.

Clearly this toad was an intellectual talent,
perhaps I should give his brain a challenge.
But what could I say that would test a toad,
sat outside my cottage, in the middle of the road?

At last I asked what at first had entered my thoughts,
How on earth was he able to talk?
He smiled politely and rose to his feet.
'Indeed I shall tell you my story, full and complete.'

He slowly removed a crown from his head.
'Without wishing to sound conceited,' he said,
'Long ago I was a normal person, just like your good self,
quite intelligent, well respected, though not of great wealth.

'I had a wife, Angelica, who was beautiful and true,
who often used to whisper, "I love you."
We lived in a cottage not dissimilar to yours,
small and neat, with roses around the door.

'Then one dark rainy day, a pedlar came to our door,
"Buy my wares my lovely and you'll be lucky for ever more.
I'll tell the fortune of your house and home."
But my wife seemed quite frightened of this old crone.

'My wife called me to her side,
her nervousness she could not hide.
Seeing her distress at the sight of this pedlar,
I did something, for me, quite out of character.

'I took an old walking stick I had in the hall,
and drove the old woman away with a mouthful of scorn.
As she quickly retreated down the lane,
she threw at me vile curses, time and again.

'I soon forgot her torrent of abuse,
which at the time seemed to amuse.
As time went by we were happy and content,
until we were blessed with a happy event.

'Oh how could anyone know such joy,
blessed with a beautiful girl and boy?
Twins, that brought double delight,
until, some time later, everything changed overnight.

'On a morning not unlike today,
I was awakened by my loved one's screams of dismay.
She was beside herself with grief,
moaning with cries and tears of disbelief.

'I raced to her side in the twins' play room,
and there to my horror I spied a scene of utter doom.
There in the middle of the floor were our beautiful offspring,
but instead of smiling faces, I saw a gruesome thing.

'Sat playing quietly in the middle of the floor,
were two of the ugliest toads I ever saw.
I gasped in horror at this hideous scene,
two ugly fat toads, round and green.

'The old pedlar woman did this, because of the fuss,
it's a curse she concocted just to get back at us.
The toad paused for a moment, as I stared in disbelief,
from his waistcoat pocket he took out a silk handkerchief.

'He dabbed a tear that appeared in the corner of his eye.
"Forgive me," he said, "I think I'm about to cry.
You see," he said, "I have not told this story to a living soul,
you always think you'll live a normal life, one of growing old."

"Is there anything that can be done?" I asked,
Wondering if this woman could be taken to task.
Then I realised he was telling me about his children's plight,
but how is it that, when he's in this state, something's not right?

"I can tell what you're thinking," he said,
as he wiped the sweat from his forehead.
"You're wondering why I am like I am,
a fat green toad, instead of a man."

"Well," he continued sadly, "I searched the land from top to toe,
for her I searched until there remained nowhere to go.
Then, by a stroke of good luck, or so I thought,
I heard of an old pedlar woman, somewhere up north.

"When I reached the place I'd been told
It was indeed the pedlar woman, grey and very old.
When she saw me she let out a cackle,
it sounded as macabre as a death rattle.

"You should not have treated me like you did,"
she said in a grisly tone. "I too needed to live."
"Surely" I said, "a curse on two souls so innocent,
was not justified in any event."

"I will grant you a way out of your dilemma,
But it must be done at the end of December
Before the last chime of the clock, at the new year,
otherwise, it will cost you dear.

'Then, with sadness, he told me what the old crone had said.
"She told him, kiss your children goodnight. Then she gasped and was dead.
Surely there is more than just that I screamed, there must be more,
But I was wasting my time, so, turning I headed for the door.

'Then' he said, 'I was about to leave, for I could do no more.
I saw her coat on a peg by the door.
As I stared at the ragged old vestment,
Sticking out of a pocket was a piece of dirty torn parchment.

'Thinking that she could have no qualms,
I took the parchment, and tucked it under my arm.
Once outside and onto the street,
I made a somewhat hasty retreat.'

The toad paused once more to mop his brow,
it was getting dark, and almost evening by now.
It seemed like a struggle for him to see,
So I asked if he'd like to come in and have some tea.

'Thank you' he said as he smiled at me,
'I would love to come in and have some tea.'
So, I led the way up a short garden path to my front door,
and of this tale I hoped to hear more.

Although it was May it was chilly outside,
so I made up the fire and bade him sit beside.
I brought in some tea and scones,
and asked him to make himself at home.

He said, 'Thank you very much for such a treat'
as he sat by the fireside warming his feet.
Before I could ask him about the rest of his story,
He began to pick up where he had left off for me.

'Where was I?' he remarked. 'About the parchment,' I added quickly,
'Oh yes,' he said slowly, 'a subject quite prickly.'
I sat forward in my chair, eagerly anticipating the next piece of the tale.
'The parchment,' he said with an agonisingly slow exhale.

'I don't know why I took the parchment,' he said thoughtfully.
'Perhaps it contained…' "A clue!" he said, finishing my sentence, airily.
Here was I chomping at the bit, so to speak,
Waiting for him to get back to the story, seemed to be taking a week.

'The parchment' he said, seeing that I was anxious for him to move on.
He began to speed up a little, not wanting to prolong.
'As I was saying,' he continued, 'That dirty old document,
It just seemed the right thing to do at that particular moment.

'The script, in a mixture of ancient texts, was quite difficult to follow,' he said.
If he doesn't get a move on, I thought, it's going to be time for bed.
'It seemed,' he went on, 'that it contained some form of incantation
Written in a strange tongue of an ancient civilisation.'

A DIVERSITY OF VERSE

'You mean a spell of some kind,' I butted in.
'Yes,' he answered, with a halfway grin.
'Fortunately, before we were married, Angelica was a teacher,
so,' he added, 'The translating was left completely to her.

'We pored over the parchment for hours,' he said in a tired tone.
'I could not have solved the puzzle all on my own.
I tried to remember,' he said thoughtfully,
'Exactly what the old crone had said to me.'

"I will grant you a way out of your dilemma,
But it must be done at the end of December
Before the last chime of the clock, to start the new year,
otherwise it will cost you dear."

'The best we could come up with, Angelica and I
was something about the liver of a cat, mixed with a rat's eye.'
Thinking the time was not late, I looked at the clock beneath a glass dome.
The hour was indeed late, surely the toad by now must on his way home.

Then it seemed, with renewed vigour, the toad carried on.
'We had just about given up,' he said with a sigh that was very long,
'When – "Eureka!" she screamed, "Obvious!" she cried in an excited tone,
"We'll save our family," she said with tears in her eyes, "Our family and home."

'What was it?' I asked, almost falling off my chair in eager anticipation.
'Angelica had translated the parchment,' he said with a smug disposition.
'She had discovered the means to undo the old crone's curse.'
'Wonderful," I said, 'But how come you didn't turn out none the worse?'

'Well,' he said sadly, 'I didn't follow Angelica's instructions to the letter.
I was far too anxious, and thought I knew better.
You remember what the old crone said?' he added, moving his chair nearer,
'The very last thing was, "otherwise it will cost you dear."

'It was entirely my fault,' he continued. 'I took a detour on the way home.
So it was almost midnight when I arrived home on new year's eve,' he droned.
'Angelica was beside herself with worry,' he said.
'The children have been asleep for hours,' she told him, 'safely tucked up in bed.'

'With that,' he said, 'the hall clock began to chime the midnight hour.
"Quick!" she whispered, not wanting to wake the children. "Time's nearly over."
We raced upstairs as quickly and quietly as we could,' he went on.
'But,' he said sadly, 'our opportunity had already gone.'

All went silent for quite a while,
it was very late as he gave a tired smile.
I could not bring myself to turn him out at such a late hour,
to have him as my guest would be an honour.

I would have to kerb my impatience until the morning,
for it was all I could do to stop myself yawning.
He thanked me warmly for my hospitality,
and bid me 'goodnight' very graciously.

I had a restless night, wondering how his story would end,
my mind was in turmoil with concern for my new friend.
I eventually dropped off into a fairly peaceful sleep,
hoping subconsciously that the solution would not be too deep.

I awoke the next morning to the sound of someone singing,
I could also hear someone at my front door the bell ringing.
Wiping the sleep from my eyes, I staggered downstairs
to find that the toad seemed to be without a care.

'Who's at the door?' I asked sleepily.
'It was me!' he said cheerfully.
'I didn't know your name,' he added.
'I thought I told you, it's Alfred.'

A DIVERSITY OF VERSE

'Sorry,' he replied with dignified humility,
'I couldn't very well shout, "hey you, breakfast's ready."'
'No,' I said, 'I'm sorry, I always wake up grumpy,
I am not used to entertaining socially.'

'What did you say about breakfast?
I cooked it for you as a late repast.'
'Late!' I stammered, 'what time is it?'
'It's almost 10 o'clock, and I must soon end my visit.'

'But,' I stammered again, 'I haven't heard your story's end.'
'There's not much more to tell you, my friend.'
'You surely can't leave it hanging there,
No, not dangling in mid-air?'

'Oh, very well,' he said, 'I'll continue while I make a drink.'
I settled myself down at the table as my cup I clinked.
'Well,' he said, 'Where was I?
Oh yes,' he answered himself. 'Opportunity!

'Do you remember what the old crone had said?' he asked.
'Yes I think so,' I said. 'It was something about a task.'
'You are close,' he replied then with a smile.
He then fell silent again for quite a while.

Finally he continued, 'You remember the clock had finished striking?'
'Yes,' I answered, without hesitation or even thinking.
'Well, when we dashed to the twins' bedroom, they were still fast asleep.
'So,' he said gravely. 'Whilst Angelica read the text, I kissed each twin upon the cheek.

'Knowing full well,' he continued. 'There was only a slim chance of success.'
'But, thank god!' he said heaving a sigh of relief. 'We were blessed.'
'I know, you are puzzled,' he said, seeing my expression,
'For a few seconds all was perfect once more,' he said, with an air of great depression.

111

'Then,' he said suddenly. 'So suddenly in fact, that I almost fell off my chair,
Angelica turned to me with a loving smile, that quickly turned to a look of fear.
"You're a t-t-t-toad!" she stammered. Dashing to the bathroom, I looked in the mirror.
I was indeed a toad.' he said sadly. 'Now my face was a picture of horror.

'It was almost sheer panic at first', he said, 'But I told myself, just calm down.
After the initial shock,' he said, 'I calmed a little, my face bore only a slight frown.'
I asked him, 'what did you do next?' He smiled and said, 'Not a lot really.
Angelica and I simply sat and cried for a while,' he answered candidly.

'The next day my wife told our friends that I had to work away for a week.
Then, at night,' he continued, 'When the kids were asleep,
'I would sneak back into the house,' he said with a broad smile.
'At least,' I said to myself, 'it will be for only a short while.

'That was of course if we, Angelica and I, could discover a solution.'
'Did you? Discover a solution I mean?' I said without consideration.
'Oh I'm terribly sorry,' I said, 'Obviously you can't have done.'
'Ah but yes, we did discover way to put things back as they were,' he went on.

'Oh dear,' I said. 'I'm forgetting my manners. It's almost one o'clock.
Would you like some lunch?' I said as I cleared the table top.
'That is most gracious of you,' he sighed.
'Not at all, you're more than welcome,' I replied.

We sat in silence and ate a light meal,
and all the while asking myself, was all this real?
After what seemed an age staring into space,
'Well, to continue,' he said, with a tired look on his face.

'When we finally decoded the parchment,' he explained,
'The solution to our problem was clear,' he claimed.
'Angelica,' he said, 'had found a solution in the text.'
'What was it?' I asked, wondering what happened next.

'Well,' he said slowly, calming my impatience
'Well,' he repeated, 'The text was indeed the answer, in essence.'
I felt like screaming, I KNOW! I KNOW! Get on with it!
But I managed to control myself and get a grip.

'Basically,' he went on, 'If we could find someone to help us of his own free will
We would indeed break the curse, 'But,' he added, 'The dangers we have to instil.
There was a serious possibility that whosoever assisted in this matter
could more than likely turn out as mad as a hatter.'

Barely had he finished when I blurted out, 'I'll help you!'
'Are you sure?' he asked. 'If so, you are a friend most true.'
'How hard can it be?' I asked, a little blasé,
not really knowing what else to say.

'What do I, or we, do?' I asked with excitement.
'First you must swear that you do willingly consent.'
'Yes, yes!' I said with rather a rude impatience,
'It will not work if you are of any indifference.'

'Right then,' said the Toad in a very businesslike manner,
'Shall we get started? Oh, by the way I need a hammer.'
'What on earth do you need a hammer for?'
Fortunately there was one just inside the garage door.

Whilst I quickly acquired a hammer he cleared the kitchen table,
thinking that he would be performing some kind ritualistic fable.
I was astonished to see it was for nothing but
the cracking of a pocket full of hazel nuts.

He smiled when he saw bemusement in my stare,
'I can concentrate better whilst eating this particular fare.'
Next he took out the dirty old parchment,
and covered it with an equally dirty old vestment.

Then, clearing his throat with a strange guttural sort of noise,
he began reciting sentences in a somewhat harmonious voice.
When he'd done he said, 'Well that's it, it's all over and I have to go home.'
'Are you sure that's it?' I asked in a puzzled tone.

'You may have some slight side effects,' he added.
'But I don't feel anything,' I said, somewhat disappointed.
'You could,' he said seriously. 'You'll have to wait about a day.'
'But I couldn't see how this would have any effect in any way.'

'So,' I said. 'What about you?
What are you going to do?'
'Nothing,' he said, 'At this moment in time.
I'm going home to tell Angelica that everything will be fine.'

'How do you mean, fine?' I asked in a worried tone.
'What will happen when you've gone home?'
'I'm not quite sure', he answered with an indifferent air.
'Please don't think,' he said, 'that I don't care.'

'I'm really not sure,' he said, in a more sympathetic tone.
'But,' he went on, 'If I were you I would stay home alone,
just to be on the safe side,' he added, with a serious frown.
'On the safe side?' I asked. 'But tomorrow I need to go into town.'

'That's out of the question,' he answered. 'Best stay at home.'
So with great reluctance I sat down and decided not to moan.
The thought of what was going to happen was going round inside my head.
Would it be so serious that I would end up dead?

That night I tossed and turned most of the time, until the early hours,
When finally I dropped off to sleep, dreaming of fields and flowers.
I awoke with something of a start, to find that it was very late morning.
Without thinking I staggered to the bathroom and began brushing my teeth, as normal

'Only to find that, to my horror, I didn't have any teeth!
Then, looking in the mirror, my horror deepened to disbelief.
'What the hell happened?' I asked myself,
Almost breaking the cabinet's glass shelf.

'In the mirror staring back at me
a sight I hoped I'd never see.
There in the mirror, a horrible scene,
was, a toad, fat, round, and very green.

'I cried out for him, the toad, realising I didn't know his name.
'Hello?' his voice enquired. 'Are you all right?'
'No, I am definitely not!' I replied harshly.
'Come in here and you will see.'

As he entered the bathroom, I got another surprise,
for there, standing before me was a, rather handsome man with pale blue eyes.
'Who are you?' I demanded.
'I'm Tobias Smithson,' he replied. 'I know I'm hard to recognise without a toad's head'.

'I am very sorry I didn't tell you my name,' he added respectfully.
'You can call me Toby, if you want to,' he said with an air of joviality.
I was in no mood for good humour.
I said, 'I trust you can get me out of this dilemma.'

'Sadly, no, I cannot. I don't know how,' he answered with his chin on his chest.
'What!' I bellowed. 'what do you mean? All this was at your behest.'
'Indeed it was, but you did agree to do it, and presumably to take any risks.'
'Yes.,' I stammered. 'But I didn't think they would be like this.'

'I have to leave now, but I will be back in a day or so.' he said turning toward the door.
'You can't leave!' I shouted. 'What am I going to do? There must be something more.'
'Stay indoors, for the time being, and I will return soon, with a solution, hopefully.'
'But how am I going to eat?' I said. 'I need some groceries.'

'All taken care of,' he answered. 'I went out early this morning and got you some.
I will speak to Angelica, to see if we can find out what can be done.
I promise I will come back with some sort of remedy,' he said, with hand on heart.
'OK' I said. We shook hands as he left, at which I felt totally alone and apart.

Three days had elapsed and, no sign of him or, even any sort of message.
I had covered all of the mirrors in the house, not bearing to see my image.
Then on the fourth day, around mid-morning, I heard the doorbell.
At first I was reluctant to answer it, but eventually I thought, what the hell?

'So I called out. 'Who's there?' 'It's me,' came the reply. 'It's Toby.'
I was so relieved I flung open the door, not expecting what I did see.
For there on my doorstep was not only Toby but a lady meek and mild.
She had long blonde hair and on each arm a beautiful child.

'I would like you to meet my wife,' he said with obvious pride.
'She has been my rock,' he added. 'Always by my side.'
'Please come in,' I said hastily, 'forgive my rudeness.'
'How have you been?' he asked, 'Not angry, I hope, for leaving you in such a mess.'

'I was, at first quite angry,' I answered. 'But then I resigned myself to my fate.
After all it was of my own choosing. So no point in getting in a state.'
'There, I told you he was a gracious fellow,' said Toby, turning to his wife.
'I think we have a true friend.' he added. 'Yes, a friend for life.'

'Pardon my manners,' I said, 'Would you like a cup of tea?'
Angelica said 'Thank you that would be very nice, no sugar for me.'
'Make yourselves at home, while I put the kettle on.'
'Not a lot has happened since you've been gone.'

'You're looking much better than the last time we spoke,' Toby remarked.
'You've got to be joking!' I muttered under my breath. 'Living in the dark.'
Toby must have realised, why and what, I was muttering.
Because he replied, 'We want you to accept this ring.'

'That's very kind of you,' I said, 'But trinkets are not what I need.'
'But this no ordinary ring,' he went on. 'It's very special indeed.'
'How so?' I asked in a disinterested tone.
'You can have anything and everything,' he said, 'without leaving home.'

'Do you mean a sort of wishing ring?' I asked
'Yes,' he said. 'One that will perform any task.'
'Will it turn me back to the man I once was?' I said.
'Why, when there is no need?' he replied with a tilt of his head.

I thought it strange that he should make such a statement.
'I can see,' he said, 'that you have no faith in my intent.'
'Well,' he said, 'look in the mirror and see what I mean.'
With great trepidation I removed a cover, expecting to see a face warty and green.

To my surprise, the face was mine and nothing did I lack.
Apart from the need for a shave, everything was back.
'How? Why? When?' I asked Toby.
'Is this really true? Is it really me?'

'Yes my friend, it's really you,' replied Toby.
Whilst all this was going on, Angelica had made the tea.
I suppose you would like to know how you changed,' said Toby.
'Well, apparently,' Angelica said, 'the old crone wasn't as bad as she was made out to be.'

'She left that ring to us in her will,' Angelica continued.
'So because of your faith in us we asked the ring for you to be renewed.
And,' she said, 'here you are back in the land of the living, so to speak.
We very much hope that you'll be a godfather to our children next week.'

'How could I refuse?' I replied.
So at the next week's christening with happiness we all cried.
That time seems so long ago now.
Although I have the ring, I find that I rarely need it somehow.

For now I have a wife of my own,
two beautiful children and a brand new home.
As the years go by I often think of T & A,
and hope that we will see them again someday.

The Traveller II

As a full moon rises high in the sky,
the air is cold and the night is still.
An owl on the wing floats silently overhead,
as a weary traveller trudges over the hill.

He feels his mind's numb because of the cold,
as he pulls his long black coat around him tight.
His journeys seem longer and longer these days,
and it's harder to keep out the chill of the night.

Trudging through the forest with trees tall and stark,
caring not for brigands and thieves
Gingerly treading a very small path,
he's not even startled by a rustle of leaves.

His past experiences have given him a sixth sense,
he seemed to know just what had made that sound.
Not fearing the dark forest at this late hour,
he knew it was only a frightened rabbit going to ground.

'Besides' he mused, 'beneath my coat I've something in which I trust,'
a weapon, he thought that would deter any would-be attacker.
Smiling, he thought of the old shotgun,
after all, it was far more than a mere firecracker.

The leaves began to rustle once more,
as he braced himself against the cold night air.
This time the breeze was gentle,
just light enough to cause the trees to stir.

Who knows what could befall someone too blind to see?
muttering to himself, 'it's not very far to go'.
Still, he thought, best to keep a look out,
so on he trudged for another mile or so.

Gathering clouds now cover the moon,
he began to stumble a little as he made his way.
It was a long time till morning,
silently wishing it was break of day.

Suddenly he was aware of a light up ahead,
as the path came to an end at a clearing.
Maybe an inn, and a place he could rest his weary bones,
the fact was, he had a very uneasy feeling.

For a few moments standing in the shadow of the trees,
there was something odd about the atmosphere.
Surveying the scene with increasing disquiet
it all was dark and foreboding, that was clear.

He stood quietly in the shadows, to the unnatural he was no stranger,
the hairs on the back of his neck bristled and stood erect.
He'd developed a keen sixth sense of impending doom,
So he hoped that the fear in his mind was only a temporary effect.

In the centre of the clearing, barely perceptible in the gloom,
stood a structure, a house, of sorts.
The structure, that appeared to be built solidly,
seem very familiar, or so he thought.

It was difficult to see, his eyesight he did bemoan,
it did not appear to be built of timber.
The structure seemed to be stone built,
Then, from somewhere in his memory, there glowed an ember.

He had seen this building, many years before,
as the clouds parted for a few seconds, the structure came to light,
The moonlight gave this scene an eerie glow.
then he remembered where he'd seen this daunting facade and, on what night.

A chill ran down his spine as he shivered,
he was not sure whether it was the cold or fear.
He was afraid that night too before being delivered,
after all, only by the grace of God was he even here.

That night, though long ago still, gave him nightmares,
this brief glimpse in the moonlight's glow
Was enough to resurrect vivid images of that scene,
how he escaped death, he will never truly know.

Once more the clouds covered the moon's eerie light,
he tentatively made his way around the edge of the clearing,
Trying to keep in the shadow of the trees.
approaching with great caution, he had a strange feeling.

As he neared the high stone wall,
memories of that night came flooding back.
Bracing himself he reached the tall wide gates,
when push came to shove, he hoped the courage he wouldn't lack.

The gates were ajar just as before,
the courtyard was empty the way it was back then in the rain.
As he quietly crossed the cold stone courtyard,
it was just as though it was happening again.

It began to rain as he reached the front of the house itself.
Half expecting what he'd seen all those years before
He gingerly pushed on the door handle,
as all those memories came pouring back once more.

He pushed the large oak door, expecting a loud screeching sound,
unlike before, the door opened smoothly, no sound at all.
Surprised by the lack of noise, he carefully stepped inside,
as he entered, the atmosphere was different in this great hall.

He had that same strange feeling that he felt he could not trace,
but this time the atmosphere's warm and dry, not cold and stark.
There seem to be more light than the last time, and, a fire ablaze in the hearth,
there was still a long candle lit staircase, that disappeared into the dark.

He thought he'd take a look around this time,
In the middle of the great hall a great oak table.
The table set for a meal, but, for only two.
a bottle of red wine, gold plates, knives, forks and placement labels.

He casually looked at the nearest placement label,
almost collapsing with shock at the sight of his own name.
He immediately started to sweat, grabbing the back of a chair for support,
all sorts of questions whirled around in his brain.

Who was there to ask and who could really answer face to face?
whilst he continued to ponder his position for a moment.
He did not notice a slight movement on the top of the stair,
in the shadows beyond the candle glow's extent.

Almost imperceptibly until, suddenly, rushing like the bursting of a dam,
a beast with bloodshot eyes and gnashing teeth.
A monstrous, fanged, drooling and foul-smelling animal,
he stared at this monster in disbelief.

At first he was stricken with shock and fear,
the beast jumped, knocking him down and then licking his face.
He quickly realised it was the beast that had saved his life that fateful year.
he was thankful back then for God's sweet grace.

Pulling at the beast's collar, he managed to get out from under the hound,
but how could this be? He had died back then.
With questions of how, why, when, rushing through his head,
he knew he'd buried him at the back of the house in the garden.

He was overjoyed to see his friend standing there fit and well,
but immediately his friend began to snarl and his neck to set.
Not noticing a second movement at the top of the stair,
just remembering their ordeal, the smell of wet dog that made him retch.

The hairs on the back of hisneck started to bristle,
not knowing the who, what, where, or why, he stood still and tense.
Straining an ear for any recognizable sound,
but all went quiet, it made no sense.

The great hall was absolutely silent save for the crackling fire,
even the hound beside him was silent in his own home.
As the thought had crossed his mind he took a sharp intake of breath,
his friend was no longer by his side, to his horror he was completely alone.

Not a sound of scampering claws on stone the floor,
no sound of any description came to his ear.
He wondered for a moment what had alarmed his friend.
He did not have to wait long; the answer was immediately clear.

As he stood rooted to the spot he felt a strange draught around his body,
there was an aroma he recognized with no surprise.
All the candles in the great hall flickered and died as if snuffed out by an unseen hand,
he silently cursed the fact the he could not see clearly because of his eyes.

Whilst holding his breath standing silently in the middle of the floor,
trying to gain a little awareness of his surroundings to clear his mind.
Then as if by magic, all the candles burst into life once again,
but now, the candles were far brighter than they were supposed to shine.

Strangely, these very bright candles were just as eerie as the dim form.
Feeling that a little of his courage had returned, he began to explore the great hall.
The new brightness lit up the tapestries and ancestral paintings of people and animals,
there were dozens of paintings hung on every wall.

As he moved around this vast space, he stayed alert for any more shocks,
moving from artefact to artefact, he began to lose interest in the images portrayed.
Until, he saw a sight, that caused him to catch his breath and disbelieve his eye's,
he glazed up at a painting that was roughly daubed and badly faded.

Although it was difficult to make out, in his mind's eye it was perfectly clear,
the faded work was unsigned but, that to him, was of no interest.
It was of his friend and him, in mortal combat with those hounds of long ago,
this work though not of great style was strangely manifest.

As he studied the work he was aware of movement behind him,
cautiously he turned around to be faced with not one, two or even three
But five hounds of hell, with that same foul smell once again permeating the air.
Four of the five were slightly smaller, the larger one was a bitch, that was plain to see.

And obvious that the smaller ones were her offspring.
He stood for what seemed ages trying to stare down these five creatures.
But the lack of aggression was a curious thing,
as he stood there he began to recognise these animal's features.

Feeling unafraid, he began to move slowly toward them,
but to his dismay, they started growling and snarling with intensity.
Obviously his tall and somewhat bedraggled form didn't cause them to retreat,
the situation was almost out of control and it was he who had to think of where to flee.

He started to back away but, immediately found himself with his back against the wall,
beads of sweat formed on his wrinkled old brow, wiping them with the cuff of his coat.
And retreating no further, he braced himself for another possible fight,
as he tried to clear his very dry throat.

Trying in his mind to formulate a plan of attack,
he said a silent prayer as the hounds crouched low and began to creep toward him.
he knew that now as before, he must not lack courage,
remembering the gun beneath his coat, he feverishly tried get it out from within.

Sensing danger, the bitch sprang at him, knocking the gun to the floor,
the gun went off, blowing a hole in one of the paintings on the wall,
Startled for a second but not for long, the bitch again sprang,
he held his breath, fully expecting to fall.

As the hound flew through the air towards him,
he thought that this night would be his last of this life.
He closed his eyes in another silent prayer,
his thoughts quickly turning to his late wife.

He thought perhaps that they would meet sooner rather than later,
for the mauling he had resigned himself to receive.
As all these emotions raced through his mind, he realised he was saved yet again,
death had passed him by once more and again he was relieved.

As he warily opened his eyes he was once again amazed at what he saw,
it appeared as if the smaller hounds were sired by, and to his friend's obvious pride,
There was no immediate danger, his friend and the bitch were side by side on the floor.
and as if to confirm the fact, his friend led the kids to his side.

With a great sigh of relief, he pulled out a chair and sat down at the table,
taking one of the goblets and the wine bottle, he poured himself a large measure.
Thinking that he would explore upstairs, as soon as he had stopped sweating,
very quickly his head began whirl, the wine had been drugged he was sure.

As he slipped into unconsciousness he was aware of someone else in the room,
as he awoke it was as bright as day.
He felt the breeze on his face and a feeling of euphoria
his head didn't seem to be where his body lay.

He lay for a moment staring at the sky,
feeling in a blissful state of mind
Watching the clouds floating overhead,
with a thousand questions and, not an answer could he find.

There was no way of telling what time of day
it could be or, even the date.
Trying to remember what had happened was
the hardest thing, he'd had to himself relate.

With his mind reeling with what had happened last night,
if, indeed, it had been last night and not a week ago.
whilst his head was aching and still very sore,
he tried to collect his thoughts on what to do and where to go.

With great difficulty he wearily got to his feet,
looking around to get his bearings.
With the sun shining in a clear blue sky,
he found himself at the edge of the clearing.

Though standing in the sunshine he still felt a coolness,
and realised he was without his coat.
Also, he was without his shotgun,
and that was his most disturbing thought.

Looking across the clearing a paleness came to his face,
there was no sign of the house at all.
Mentally checking that this was indeed where the house had stood,
as he attempted to clear his mind, the rain began to fall.

RON STEELE

At first he took no notice, but then he realised the sky wasn't clear,
it must have clouded over in a blink of an eye.
He tried to shelter under a larger pine tree that was close,
but it didn't afford much shelter, being far too high.

Being distracted by the rain he tried to focus on now,
rather than last night, or whenever that was.
His mind was starting to whirl a little whilst he was standing there wondering,
how he'd got to here in the state he was.

He couldn't really think straight being cold and in the rain,
so he wandered back into the forest hoping to find some meaning.
At least beneath this thick canopy he had shelter.
Shivering, he slapped his upper arms trying to regain a little feeling.

As he made his way through the trees,
he realised it was late in the day
If he told his story who would believe him,
changing his direction through the forest might be a better way.

Shrugging his already drenched shoulders he trudged on warily,
where to, he did not exactly know.
For it seemed all of his get up and go had already got up and gone.
and now it felt like his legs were being dragged through two feet of snow.

It was now almost dark but with a full moon lighting his way,
he trudged on, then, became aware of a light up ahead.
It seemed like deja vu, had he walked in a circle?
no way could he fathom what was happening inside his head.

As he stood once again on the edge of the clearing,
there, standing stark in the moonlight.
He could not believe his eyes,
the stone edifice, where he had been the previous night.

As he tried to take in what was happening,
he thought, it's a dream, but instantly, a cold shiver ran through his body.
Still wet through, still standing in the rain,
wondering whether or not to chance going back for the sake of curiosity.

After all his friend, and indeed his friend's family, might need him,
he could not in all conscience leave, that would be a sin.
So gathering what little mental fortitude he had, he set off back,
by the time he arrived the front door, he was soaked to the skin.

On arrival at the front gate he was somewhat perturbed,
the door was different, it wasn't wood, instead it was made of metal.
The large ornate knocker was replaced by a small notice which read
'He who strikes this door does so at his own peril'.

He chose to simply ignore the notice and push the great door,
to his surprise, nothing happened.
No matter how much effort he put in, it didn't move,
how was he supposed to gain entry to aid his friend?

He thought one more push, still nothing,
mentally scratching his head, he had an idea.
So he made his way around house,
to see if he could gain an entry at the rear.

As he made his way around to the rear of the house,
he came across what looked like a walled garden.
He walked the entire length of the wall, it did not seem to have any means of entry,
he was about to give up when the thought of his friend made him try again.

The wall seemed to be of great age,
and its surface was made of rough-hewn stone.
There were plenty hand and footholds,
he managed to climb to the top even though he was chilled to the bone.

Sitting for a moment to get his breath back atop the garden wall,
he surveyed the scene below, taking in his surroundings.
Feeling that it was safe, he descended quietly, trying not to stumble.
Once on the ground he looked around to regain his bearings.

At the back of the house he could make out a light,
it was shining from an upstairs room.
Moving to his right and trying to keep a low profile,
he then quietly made his way across a roughly cut lawn.

Reaching what he thought must be a kitchen door,
he carefully lifted the latch, luckily, it moved freely.
Holding his breath, he slowly pushed the door open,
heaving a sigh of relief as it opened silently.

As quietly as he could he stepped through the door,
and closed it behind him, thinking that it might bang in the wind.
As he adjusted his eyes to the gloom, a shiver ran right through him
Where should he go now, he pondered, searching his mind.

First things first he finally thought, 'upstairs is maybe where the answers are'.
Moving as quietly as he could he crossed the kitchen floor.
Thinking all was not well, he began to feel the pounding of his heart,
he crossed to far side of the kitchen and quietly opened the door.

To his relief the great hall was deserted and as though nothing had happened,
and his blunderbuss was propped up against a dining chair.
His coat was draped over the back of another at the end of the table,
everything seemed to be too quiet, like stepping into a monster's lair.

He cautiously crept forward towards his gun,
looking left and right, checking for signs of movement of any kind.
He crossed the great hall and was about to pick up his weapon
when he heard a noise behind him, and a thousand thoughts ran through his mind.

Spinning swiftly around, he saw with great relief his friend standing behind him,
He turned back to pick up his gun and his coat.
But to his horror they were gone from the chair,
A violent shiver ran through his body and his dry throat.

Turning yet again his horror continued,
his friend had also disappeared with no trace.
Wondering if he was dreaming, he began to be a little confused,
Beads of perspiration began forming on his face.

He began to feel faint, hot, and disoriented,
And sitting down at the table he tried to dispel the trials of the day.
At least it was warm and dry in the great hall,
Warm and dry, but how? the fire was still blazing away.

How could the fire keep going on its own?
The only explanation was that there is someone else here.
But who, what or where, and is it he or she,
He sat trying to make some sense and his mind to clear.

After he had sat pondering what was his best plan,
he decided to take the bull by the horns.
Rising quickly, he strode purposely toward the staircase,
pausing for a second at the bottom, he felt suddenly all alone.

So taking a deep breath, he made his way cautiously up the stairs,
not knowing who or what he'd find, he pressed on.
As he climbed he was aware of his footfalls echoing all through the house,
He decided not bother about the noise, the time to worry was long gone.

On reaching the top he could see that there were several long corridors,
each one going off in a different direction from the landing.
Standing in the poor light he was uncertain as to which one he should to take,
While making up his mind he heard a muffled sound, but from where was it coming?

It seemed to emanate from down the corridor to his immediate left,
so, he thought, in for a penny in for a pound.
There were numerous doors off this corridor, presumably all bedrooms.
As he walked on he wished he had the company of his friend the hound.

Checking each door as he went, finding each one locked,
Just as he was about to turn back and try another corridor.
A room to his right he found was unlocked,
slowly turning the handle, he opened the door.

The door hinges creaked a little as the door swung open.
as he stood there in the doorway he was amazed by what he saw.
The whole room was decorated in gold, gold everywhere,
he had never seen so many gold ornaments in his life before.

After a while he realised he was standing with his mouth agape,
he mentally shook himself and started to look around.
Carefully he lifted them, each appeared to be priceless objet d'art.
It seemed this was a treasure chest he had found.

'Wait a minute', he thought, this is someone's property,
I haven't found anything' he mused.
As he stared in wonder at this fabulous wealth,
something caught his eye, on a dressing table that was somewhat unused.

It was almost covered by all the gold clutter,
He very gently picked it up and lifted it to the light.
It was a simple but strange fine gold chain necklace,
But it was the pendant that was strange on this already strange night.

The pendant was very familiar,
it was identical to the one he had given to his wife so dear.
Logically speaking there must be literally thousands of these about,
How could this have, if indeed it was hers, turned up here?

As he twirled the teardrop pearl pendant in the candle light,
he remembered there was a small flaw in the back of the bead.
He smiled when he remembered how she had teased him about it,
saying how cheap it must have been.

As he turned the bauble, he found himself wishing it was not hers,
But a cold child went through his whole being, freezing his senses.
When he realised this was that very same gift,
He had given her as an anniversary present.

As he sat at the ornate dressing table remembering his beloved,
He was suddenly aware of a slight sound behind him.
He spun swiftly around to face whatever it was,
But there was nothing and no one there, just silence as the lights dimmed.

Then, faintly in the distance, he heard a familiar rumble,
it sounded as though a storm was brewing.
For a moment he was distract by the distant rumble,
But he quickly brought himself back to what he was doing.

He rose from the dressing table very cautiously,
clutching the fine gold chain securely in his hand, he was not putting this back.
Moving slowly and as quietly as he could, he reached the bedroom door,
Just as he crossed the threshold, he almost had a heart attack.

There standing almost silently in the dimly-lit corridor
were his friends who immediately began growling,
But at who or what? Whilst he pondered on who or what,
a bright flash lit up the whole of the landing.

This flash was almost immediately followed by a massive rumble,
the storm arrived quickly, he thought, with very bright lightning
At the end of the corridor was an enormous stained glass window,
and framed in the window was a figure that was startling.

Could this be the person he sensed just before passed out?
he couldn't really tell, after all he had been losing consciousness to be fair.
As he contemplated his position there was another flash,
and a quick glance showed him that the man was no longer there.

He had gone in an instant, but where?
His friends began creeping forward, snarling as they went.
Within seconds there was another massive flash,
With an equally massive rumble, the window was completely rent.

He had barely time take a breath when his friends
leapt through the air at what appeared to be nothing but fresh air.
In less than a heartbeat all six of them seemed to be frozen in time.
And in suspended animation, statuesque, as it were.

He could not believe his eyes, after all he had seen this was the strangest,
then the thought crossed his mind that he was affected in the same way.
To his relief, he found that he could move quite freely,
another flash, followed by one immediately after, lighting the scene as bright as day.

In the extra time it was light, he could see his friends clearly
he could also see, framed against the window, the man.
He had his hands outstretched, as though pointing with all of his fingers,
there appeared to be electrical charges emanating from his hands.

The charges seemed to be holding his friends, with pained expressions,
about two feet off the ground, suspended in their actions.
Without thinking he picked up a large vase on an occasional table just to his right,
and hurled it in the direction of the tall figure, hoping perhaps to cause a distraction.

In a flash the man's attention turned to the vase flying towards him through the air,
in the same instant his friends were released from the man's grip.
Being released they continued their flights through the air,
Knocking the tall figure backwards towards the window, causing him to slip.

Under the considerable combined weight of the hounds the man crumbled
He began slipping and sliding backwards across the polished wooden floor.
With an enormous crash he went straight through the stained glass window,
falling through the air, his screaming could just be heard above the hounds' roar.

In the briefest of moments it was all over, as the storm rumbled away into the distance
all went silent, but, what about his friends? What would he find?
He rushed over to the window expecting to see Lord knows what
but on looking down through the broken glass, was baffled to see not a sign.

He could see nothing of the man or his friends,
just broken glass scattered on the rain-soaked lawn.
Suddenly there was a near eerie silence,
All he could hear was the faintest of rumbles in the early dawn.

As he stood in the space that had been a window,
he couldn't help thinking that, once again, his friend had made the ultimate sacrifice.
But, in the back of his mind, he couldn't help feeling that, this wasn't the case,
after all, his friend had returned after appearing to have paid the ultimate price.

Perhaps he would again return.
With a heavy heart he turned and trudged wearily back down the corridor.
Down at the bottom of the staircase he crossed the great hall,
picking up his coat and his gun, he turned towards the front door.

He hadn't taken but a few steps when he heard a familiar sound,
Looking up to the top of the staircase, he saw a sight that gladdened his heart.
It was his friend, with, his family by his side,
It seemed they were destined not to part.

With a lot of unanswered questions going around in his head,
he decided to leave this weird place.
Outside, the rain was still falling,
it felt very refreshing running down his tired, wrinkled face.

Closing the front gates behind him, he turned for one last look
and could believe his eyes yet again.
Where the house had stood was just an empty space,
Save for two gravestones, standing silent in the pouring rain.

As he read the inscriptions on the stones,
he couldn't tell if there were tears or the rain running down his face.
After all he had endured in his life, this was the hardest to take,
He had found his wife's, and friend's, last resting place.

As he reached the edge of the clearing he took one last look back,
there, through the pale morning light.
he wasn't sure if what he was seeing for real,
or if it was just his poor eyesight

There, where the house had stood,
was what appeared to be the figure of a woman alone
Save for several hounds at her feet.
He wiped the rain and the tears from his eyes and looked again, but they were gone.

After a while trudging down the path,
he realised the rain had stopped and the sun was shining.
With the sun on his back and a spring in his tired legs,
He thought, what a wonderful life for living.

Thinking time

We do not feel the summer's breeze,
nor heed the lark's sweet song
We never notice nature's gifts,
whilst in the modern throng.

Nowhere is there a permanence,
or any standards kept
A throwaway world is what we have,
where every virtue aside is swept.

This rushing world no scruples has
or sense of inner pride
It only worries about profit or loss,
or will the market slide?

We know the world cannot stand still
and man must strive to improve his lot
But honour, truth and nature's gifts
must never be forgot.

A changing world must carry forth
the values of its past
Never standing idly by,
whilst they're trampled in the dust.

If we do not protect the things we love,
we cannot truly forward move
There'll always be a hell on earth,
and never a heaven above.

So before each day is finally o'er
we must be true and do the best we can,
And always find within one's heart,
to forgive the sins of one's fellow man.

Weep not for me

Weep not for me a teary eye,
for I'll be not sorrowful when I die.
I've had, for me, a wonderful life,
with a beautiful girl who became my wife.

We've had fifty years of wedded bliss,
it's true we've had times that were amiss.
But after all those years that we've been through,
her love for me has been ever true.

I cannot believe that in my life this late,
I am deserving of such a fate.
Still, lucky in love it's often said,
comes from the heart and not from the head.

But with each passing day,
I love you more in every way.
Do not for me grieve long and deep,
nor for me go without a night's sleep.

Kiss our children and grandchildren goodbye,
tell them I love them, and not to cry.
I will not be entirely gone,
for the love we share will live on and on.

Place for me a flower upon where I lie,
and weep not for me a teary eye.
So my love, in my life I have but one regret,
that my passing causes your grief, my dearest darling Margaret.

Who cares?

When you're small and the world seems a frightening place,
who cares enough to wipe a tear from your face?
If you fall and take the skin from your knee,
who cares enough to say 'come here, let me see'?

As the years pass and your confidence grows,
who cares enough to point the way you should go?
Even after the time when from home you go,
who cares enough to tell you things you don't know?

After many years have passed and you feel you are wise,
it's your turn to care for those tender grey eyes.
It's never a chore when all's said and done,
to care for the one who cared for you, your mum.

Winter bygone

Rainy streets and dark grey skies,
runny noses and tear filled eyes
The leaves that are left are withered and brown,
winter's not here yet, but the old folks frown.

Too wet to go and play in the park,
we no longer hear the song of the lark.
Watching the rain form rings in the pools,
hoping it will stop before it's time for school.

Those school days were not so bad,
we didn't think of how little we had.
Of what we owned we made the best,
even right down to the holes in our vests.

Woolly gloves that went baggy when wet,
Balaclava helmets that went soggy with breath.
We'd tramp to school in the pouring rain,
sometimes still wet, we'd tramp home again.

Each day seemed colder than the one before,
could it really be too cold for snow?
Then at last, that day would come,
that carpet of white that brought so much fun.

On with our wellies and outside we dash,
slipping and sliding in the snow we'd crash
Playing for hours in those icy streets,
with frozen ears, hands, noses and feet.

After hours of fun and our clothes soaking wet,
a fireside's the place you never forget.
Heat from the fire gave our fingers hot ache,
but Oxo was the cure that mum would make.

In front of the fire glowing outside and in,
the shine on the stove came from out of a tin.
That polished look was known as black lead,
it would always remind me of bath and bed.

In an old tin bath in front of the grate,
on Saturday nights, I could stay up late.
Once clean and fresh and hair combed right,
I'd be allowed to listen to 'In Town Tonight'.

Neighbours and friends would come in from next door,
drinking tea and chatting about that radio show.
I'd listen for ages to what the adults said,
I didn't really want to go off to bed.

'The Man in Black' was a radio show,
Light Programme, around ten o'clock or so.
We'd listen to a man called Valentine Dyall,
thinking of it now, it makes me smile.

Getting up early to go to school,
on a weekday was the golden rule.
At weekends I never was early to bed,
as a treat, Saturday night I'd stay up instead.

Sunday morning I'd eagerly wait
for the paper man, who was always late.
He'd pedal round the terrace on an old shop bike,
a basket full of comics, had this man called Mike.

RON STEELE

Rain, hail or shine, he'd stop at our door,
with lots of comics, we'd buy three or four.
With these small treats we felt truly blessed,
even if we did have holes in our vests.

He'd ask my dad if he'd seen the game,
but sadly, dad's answer was almost always the same
he hardly ever got to see his beloved rugby league,
a seven-day a week man with a family to feed.

Eight-hour shifts, then sometimes twelve,
he worked so hard with no thought of himself.
Time was precious there was no doubt,
many years later time found him out.

The only Saturday he ever had free,
he gave it up for the chance to come and watch me.
He'd never seen me play for my school,
no time to watch football was usually the rule.

For my dad to watch I felt was a real treat,
early at the bus stop is where our team would meet.
We piled on the bus without a care,
they all thanked my dad for paying the fare.

A bright sunny day with a frost on the ground,
a glistening white carpet lay all around.
We arrived at the pitch and were filled with dismay,
the ground was too hard to play that day.

We grumbled and moaned and begged to start,
not caring if our knees would be torn apart.
My dad agreed that the teacher was right,
the frost was too keen throughout the night.

And so with sadness we returned on the bus,
my dad once again paid for all of us.
He never did have the time again,
to even watch me play in the rain.

That year we were champions, only losing one game,
but without my dad, it wasn't the same.
I wonder if he'd have been proud that day,
if he'd have been able to watch me play.

I'm sure he was proud all through my teens,
I hope I fulfilled his hopes and dreams.
He always said I should have a trade,
not making my way with shovel and spade.

I would like to think if he could see me now,
there'd be a smile beneath that wrinkled brow.
Lots of things I should have said and done,
not knowing time was precious, and now it's all gone.

No time for me to say what I felt,
no way to change the hand he was dealt.
No way to turn back life's clock,
just be thankful for all the things that we got.

When I think back to the way I would feel,
I often wonder if it was all real.
So, instead I pray to heaven above,
that my Pops looks down with a face full of love.

This small peep into my world as a kid was born out of the love I felt and still feel to this day, for a wonderful man, my late father, Matt Steele.

A summer's daydream

Rose petals heavy with a dewy kiss,
sunlight streaming through the leafy boughs
Two eyes sparkling as do limpid pools,
to me, it's heaven right here, right now.

The morning mist lingers atop a grassy knoll,
slightly swirling as doth a spirit form.
The sounds of the morning upon the still air,
make this a scene of my heart and home.

A stream over stones gurgles away,
it sparkles like diamonds from hidden depths.
As a forest nymph from a leafy glade,
across water-splashed stones lightly steps.

This fairy creature with a magical glow
dances through the grass with skilful grace.
Through sunbeams of the morn she gleefully skips,
an enigmatic smile upon her elfin face.

A gentle breeze then stirs the leaves,
and carries the song from a lark on high.
I gaze above in wonder and in awe
at cotton-bud clouds against an azure sky.

Amid this peaceful woodland scene
where everything it seems is in its place.
I lie and absorb the sounds all around,
and imagine the smile upon your face.

A cool wind rises, and the fairies flee
as darkening clouds start to fill the sky
The sunlit scene becomes dark and grey,
as thunder is heard, and a storm is nigh.

As the rain starts to fall in stair-rod form,
I try find shelter from the torrent above
As the lightning flashes through the trees,
I should be by the side of my love.

Then, almost as quickly as it came,
the storm passes me by.
The sun shines bright once again,
from out of a clear blue sky.

Sparkling raindrops upon leaves do hang,
glistening like jewels all around.
A rainbow with colours of red, blue, green and gold,
high in the sky yet seemingly, right down to the ground.

The sound of the storm is now barely heard,
its distance so far removed.
Everything in the woodland is returning to a tranquil state,
and I can once again dream of my love.

Her face is sweeter than an elfin gaze,
her smile like the morning sun.
She is the most precious thing in my life,
without whose help I could not have done what I have done.

It is with wonder that I view my life,
and all that I possess and own.
It would be a waste of time and space,
without you to make our house a home.

No matter how I fantasize
about what could be, and seem,
There is no doubt that without you here,
my life would be, just a dream.

Anguish of a dream

I dreamed a dream I can't recall,
I wonder, did I ever dream at all?
Flights of fancy that seemed surreal,
no way of explaining the way I feel.

At times when I'm tired they come, I find,
from the deepest, darkest, depths of my mind.
Haunted, my mind is rent in two,
with these demons loose, what should I do?

If I should lose control of my will,
driven by dreams that would do me ill
For me, there would be nought to my life,
no reason or rhyme, only sorrow and strife.

If that day ever came when I could not decide
where my mind did live or my soul reside
Then with great pains which one should I choose,
My mind to save, or my soul to lose?

So if my life I did freely take
I'd forfeit my soul for my mind's sake.
My soul would know no peace at all,
because of a dream I couldn't recall.

So, be not only aware of ghouls in the night,
but bad dreams too, that make a soul take flight.
Always have faith in heaven above,
and your soul will be safe with the one you love.

Conflicts

In the lull of the battle, when no shrapnel flies
and the silence seems just as deafening
That's a time when tired, tear-filled eyes
look toward the heavens in a hope of an infinite meaning.

'Up to one's neck in muck and bullets'
never seemed so apt, in this arena of uncertainty.
Brief moments of rest between the conflicts
is the way we try to regain a semblance of sanity.

Sitting in pools of rainwater stained with blood
hoping the shells will pass us by
Everywhere you look there's a sea of mud,
and above us, a sunless grey sky.

Cries of the wounded tear at one's soul,
comrades lost in no-man's land.
Thankful to have no wounds at all,
surely by the grace of God's hand.

So many lives lost for nothing it seems,
so many with no future at all.
So many men without a dream,
why did so many have to fall?

When will we learn that life is a precious gift?
if we never learn, then we will never know peace.
So do we fight until there's no one left,
or do we find a way to make the conflicts cease?

Parkinson's (the curse)

It's not life-threatening, or so they say,
but they don't live with it every day.
frustrations of life in the weirdest constrictions
when your body is controlled by mindless decisions.

Your personality's been altered beyond recognition,
and there's no way to make amends for the slightest indiscretion.
No way to do what you want to do,
you're trapped in a body that a mind won't work for you.

Quality of life is not an outrageous request for your life's duration,
just peace of mind within a body of reasonable coordination.
To move unaided, to speak clearly and the ability to swallow,
just small insignificant things to most that your body won't allow.

It's hard for those around you to understand what is meant,
what goes on in your head, when confused messages from the brain are sent.
Just peace of mind is all one asks,
to be able to complete the simplest of tasks.

So please, consider me not a weird nutcase of some kind,
all I require is a little consideration and patience from time to time.
Because the speed at which I think is not to me so crucial,
to you it may seem an eternity, but to me it's terminal.

I never thought that this life I live to me would be so hard,
rebuke me for whinging so, and playing the sympathy card.
But it's difficult to do other than
when one has been an active man.

I know there'll be a cure one day,
and soon, I hope and pray.
It will not come soon enough for me,
or the quality of life I may not see.

To whinge a little helps to ease the pain,
as I say to myself time and again.
There are many more people worse off than you,
so get on and do what you have to do.

At my end I hope there'll be,
a quiet resting place for me.
till then I will bear with all the good grace that I can
this nuisance curse called Parkinson's.

Remembrance

Blood-stained muddy puddles,
Rain-soaked muddy boots
Never knowing where its coming from,
that final scream or shout.

Deafening sound of gunfire
numbs the very brain.
When the guns are silent,
all you can here is the fall of the rain.

Up to your neck in muck and bullets,
or so the saying goes.
Only the high and mighty officers
make sense of the to's and fro's.

For the ordinary soldier in the trenches,
far from hearth and home
No one to comfort the dying,
so many died alone.

But for every soul a prayer is said,
for every soul, even you and me.
No longer in physical pain or torment,
only peace for a soul set free.

When eventually the guns are silenced
and those who are left go home
Will they have a hero's welcome,
the ones whose lives are no longer whole?

A body can heal its wounds,
but a mind cannot do the same.
It's simple to mend a broken leg,
but you can't always mend a damaged brain.

So on remembrance day, waving banners and flags,
remember too those who did not die.
On that battle field far away,
but try to live their lives as best they can, with only a tear to cry.

The last poppy petal

When the last poppy petal has fallen
and the air is cold and still
you may hear a lone piper,
atop a distant hill.

His haunting refrain may be heard above
former battlefields ravaged and torn
Especially now the guns are silent,
and all living have gone home.

He plays his pipes for all those souls
who will never see another dawn
For they are in a better place,
where heaven they'll now call home.

For those whose lives will continue on,
there will always be a place
Where they can find some solitude,
outside the world's rat race.

A place where we can quietly reflect,
on what might or might not have been
Not in the mad relentless rush,
but in peaceful fields of green.

So when the ghosts of comrades past
invade your troubled sleep
Remember them with reverence,
and to your heart their memory keep.

When the last poppy petal has fallen
and the air is cold and still
You may perchance hear a lone piper,
atop that distant hill.

When you dream

When you dream, do you dream of castles in the air,
and of long ago those knights so bold?
Do you dream of damsels fair?
or of scary stories that you've been told?

When you're a child you often dream
of things that are of no great significance.
Probably just of sweets and ice cream,
and never things like high finance.

Thoughts of a child can be complex too, we hear,
worrying about all sorts of things adults would not.
Whether they'll get a visit from Santa this year,
or if the weather is going to be cold or hot.

All things to a child are important it's true,
like tenderness, caring and love.
Knowing nothing about why the sky and the sea are blue
or whether there's a heaven above.

To be a child is a special time
to live your life with no malice or greed.
To take life as it comes, without reason or rhyme,
would be, for an adult, perfection indeed.

So if you find as time goes by
that your children severely try your patience
So much so that there comes a teary eye,
be not so downcast with nerves that are taut and tense.

Because you know that in your heart of hearts,
there will be a day not too far into the future
When your whole world's about to fall apart,
the smile on your teenager's face says that your love couldn't be purer.

www.ingramcontent.com/pod-product-compliance
Lightning Source LLC
Chambersburg PA
CBHW061655040426
42446CB00010B/1742